BRINGING UP A FAMILY
THE TEEN YEARS

'Bringing up a family,' says Mary Batchelor, 'is the greatest single experiment in life.' Drawing on a wealth of expert advice in addition to her own experience as a teacher and mother of three, she packs this guide full of helpful, practical information for parents facing this hazardous but rewarding job.

Each stage has its own joys and problems. Whether you're trying to cope with your son or daughter's puberty, church attendance or unemployment, *Bringing up a Family* helps you assess what are the really important factors to bear in mind, and lets you know where specialist help is available. And from her own experience, the author emphasizes the need for family life to be based on a living Christian faith.

Bringing up a Family
THE TEEN YEARS

MARY BATCHELOR

A LION GUIDE
Tring · Belleville · Sydney

Published by
Lion Publishing Corporation
10885 Textile Road, Belleville, Michigan 48111, USA
ISBN 0 85648 818 6

First edition 1981
Second edition 1983
This edition 1985

Acknowledgments
Edited for US edition by Evelyn Bence
Illustrations by Ron Ferns and Kathy Wyatt
Cover photograph by Pictor International

Author's note
For some reason we have no word in English to
mean both 'he' and 'she'. So it has been the
custom to say 'he' and 'him' when a writer does
not know the sex of the person referred to. I
have—rather regretfully—followed this
practice. After all, it would be just as unfair
to say 'she' throughout. But I do apologize to
all proud parents of daughters and trust that they
will understand that girls are included just as
much as boys. Just change the 'he' to 'she' as
you read!

Printed and bound in Great Britain by
Cox and Wyman Ltd, Reading

CONTENTS

SETTING THE SCENE 7

GROWING UP 13

EDUCATION 21

BEING A TEENAGER: WHAT'S IT ALL ABOUT? 32

HOME AND . . . 49

THE EVERYDAY BUSINESS OF LIVING 62

IN TROUBLE? 73

WHAT NEXT? 82

INDEPENDENCE 93

JOB COMPLETED? 104

SOME USEFUL ADDRESSES 111

INDEX 112

SETTING
THE SCENE

Which of the following comments would *you* check as correct?

- **A** Baby days are the happiest days for parents
- **B** They may be hard work when they're tiny but they're far more worry when they get to their teens
- **C** **Every** stage of bringing up a family has its problems and its joys

Let's hope that, deep down, you agree with C, though at present you may be hitting a bad patch with your own particular child (children) and be feeling that things are getting harder as he gets older.

How can this book help? It's intended as a guide. A guided tour of a building usually aims to show you the lie of the land, as in a new school, or to point out the beauties of the place, as in a stately home. A manual for some new machinery warns of possible dangers and problems. This guide hopes to do a bit of all of these things. Being prepared in advance is half the battle, and being made aware of some of the fun and enjoyment of family life, as well as the problems it may bring, can stand you in good stead. Knowing that what is happening in your family is perfectly normal can be reassuring too, should you be in the midst of a crisis. Here are some other things the guide aims to give:

- **INFORMATION** On health, education, youth organizations and a host of other family concerns, with names and addresses of groups or societies that can give further help or support and details of helpful booklets
- **BELIEF** What you believe affects how you run your family. This guide looks at the family from the Christian viewpoint
- **AIMS** Thinking about your aims and methods as well as your relationship with your children matters very much

SNAGS!

There are snags in writing a family guide when no two families are alike. What may be true for your family almost certainly won't be for the family next door. Think of all the possible variations:

DIFFERENT
- parents: marriage relationship
- children: even those in the same family are quite unique
- composition: number of children/grandparents living in
- circumstances: town or country/well-off or hard up/both at work or neither

No guide can be precise without giving the impression that all good families should be cast in the same mold. There will be bits of the book that don't fit into *your* family circumstances, so skip them and make use of what suits your situation and experience.

DON'T TAKE IT AS GOSPEL

The other main snag concerns the writer. Who can claim to know *all* about bringing up a family or lay down the law of dos and don'ts? I certainly can't! I am an ordinary mother who made plenty of mistakes in bringing up our own daughter and sons. But I have supplemented my own experience with advice and views of specialists in many fields, whether education, health, or whatever. And I have included the teaching of the

Bible about family life. *That* you can take as gospel! For the rest, you may disagree with the personal views, but at least that will help you to think more carefully about your own beliefs and aims.

WHAT ARE YOU AIMING FOR?

When I was first learning to ride a bike my aunt advised me to look straight ahead at the point I aimed to reach—at the other end of the garden path! That way, I'd stop wobbling and go straight there. We don't always reach the goals we aim for, but we stand a much better chance if we know what we're aiming at and keep our eye on that. Now that junior days are over and your son (or daughter) is growing up, what kind of person do you want him to grow into?

- someone who thinks for himself

or

- someone who thinks as you do

- someone who gets to the top

or

- someone who cares for others on the way

- a good leader of others

or

- a good follower

- one who fits in with others

or

- one who stands out in the crowd

GROWING PLANTS

'May our sons in their youth be like plants that grow up strong,' exclaims the poet who wrote Psalm 144 in the Bible. Behind the poetry is good solid truth. If you have indoor plants, or garden ones, you know what they require: feeding, watering, warmth, light, protection from disease, encouragement and care. You also know that too much fussing kills them: more indoor plants are killed by overwatering than by neglect. All these rules apply to bringing up children. You also know the obvious fact that however well you care for a plant, it is only capable of growing into the best of its kind. A maidenhair fern won't produce scarlet geranium flowers, nor will a bushy plant become a climber. Each plant makes good and develops according to its own nature and no one moans at a plant for lacking the characteristics of a quite different variety.

The same should be true of children. It's right that parents should have character aims. Every parent wants to see truthfulness, kindness and a host of other virtues flourish in their children. But it's not fair to have goals that involve their developing into the kind of people they were never intended to be. A father who has always been a 'yes man' may long for a

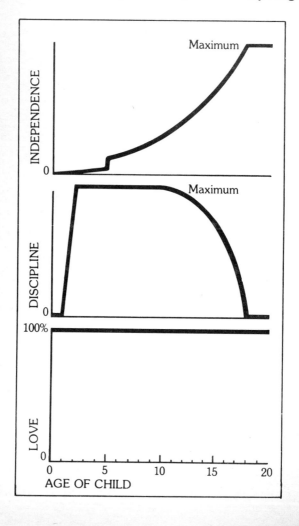

son who will be a leader of men. A mother who had no chance of higher education may want her daughter to go to university and be a career woman. But children aren't here in order to fulfil parents' own unrealized ambitions. The training and upbringing they receive should enable them to develop into the kind of people they are designed to be, reaching fulfilment according to their own nature and ability.

HOW IS IT DONE?

As they grow up, children need love, discipline and independence. These three are needed by older children just as much, though perhaps in slightly different proportions. As the graph shows, only love stays constant. Children need love from the moment they are born for as long as parents are alive to give it.

The new-born baby has no independence, but soon grows into a toddler who wants to do things for himself. Parents must begin to let their child go from the time he starts school or even earlier, and continue to 'lengthen the reins' as they see he is ready, until he is able to cope completely on his own.

Discipline begins as soon as the small child is old enough to pit his own will against his parents', but as he grows older, they try to bridge the gap from parent-control to self-control, so that by the time he is grown-up, discipline from outside becomes self-discipline.

Although this book is concerned with many practical matters, it is also concerned to work out how to keep these three in right proportion during the years from ten to eighteen or more:

- **LOVE** How to go on feeling it and showing it in a way he'll understand and appreciate
- **DISCIPLINE** How to know what rules to impose and how to enforce them
- **INDEPENDENCE** At what stage to let him fend for himself

MODELS TO COPY

Looking at the way that other people have coped can sometimes help, but it can also be confusing or disheartening. But a vital clue to our behavior as parents can be found in the way that God treats us. In the Bible, God is pictured as Father-plus-Mother. Unfortunately most people think of God as entirely masculine, yet mother as well as father images are used about him. Isaiah compares God looking after his people to a mother bird caring for her young. Jesus himself described his feelings towards the men and women of his day as being like those of a mother hen who longs to gather all her chicks under the safety of her wings. Pictures of God as Father come many times over.

So how does God act in love, discipline and giving of independence towards his children?

- **LOVE** God never stops loving us, however we behave and whatever we do. That's not to say he doesn't care when we are selfish, greedy or cruel. Real love means caring a great deal.
- **DISCIPLINE** The Bible says that God disciplines every true son of his. He corrects and punishes when necessary—but always for our good, which is more than can be said on all occasions about the punishments that human parents dish out!
- **INDEPENDENCE** God has created us free people, able to make up our own minds whether to love and obey him or to disregard him and go our own way. That's a model worth following. As children grow up, they gradually must stand free of their parents and choose their own values and their own way in life.

GROWING UP

It may seem like yesterday when *he* was in his high chair or *she* was taking her first steps but it's only too obvious that they are beginning to grow up. In fact, as far as body changes go, boys and girls are growing up at an even earlier age than they were a generation ago.

THE PHYSICAL FACTS

The word 'puberty' is used to describe the age at which a boy's or girl's body develops to be capable of having children of their own. Today they often reach this stage before they enter junior high and certainly many years before they are ready in any other way to start their own family.

It's important that a child should be told well in advance about the changes that will happen to him or to her, so that there need be no fear or anxiety when they do occur. In the upper elementary grades most schools provide films or information in other ways about sex, and the teacher may call parents together to discuss the material he will use or write to tell them about the film they plan to show. Parents are sometimes invited to be present. The girls are usually shown a film on menstruation and feminine hygiene.

But whether the school provides information or not, make sure that *you* do. If you have always found it easy to talk to your child about the 'facts of life', you may not find it difficult now to give him the help he needs. If you feel too embarrassed to go into all the details, it is better to explain what you can and give him a book to supply the rest.

WHAT AGE?

What is true about every other part of growing up is true of puberty too. There is no right age for it to happen; in fact, there is a wide range of times at which a child may reach puberty and be *normal*. Children who feel behind the times may be worried or feel self-conscious, as may early developers, so they need plenty of reassuring that they are perfectly normal. Should *you* be worried, have a word with your doctor. The usual ages are from nine to fourteen for girls and from twelve to fifteen for boys. (Note that this is about two years later than for girls.)

WHAT HAPPENS?

At puberty, the child's body begins to change into an adult's. The changes don't all happen at once or in any fixed order. But these are the main changes you can tell them to expect:

BOYS
- grow taller, shoulders broaden
- penis gets larger
- hair grows under arms, between legs, on face and chest
- sweating begins
- voice 'breaks': becomes lower
- spots, acne (more likely than for girls)
- erections more frequent, 'wet dreams' occur

GIRLS
- grow taller
- breasts develop
- hair grows under arms, between legs
- sweating begins
- menstruation: monthly periods begin
- spots or acne are likelier

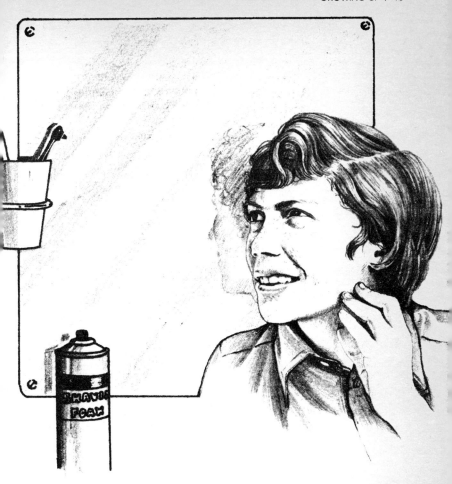

'THERE'S NOTHING WRONG'

BOYS A boy may feel self-conscious because he has the beginnings of a moustache, or because there is no sign of such a thing when all his mates are complaining about shaving. But it's the more private happenings that may cause the most worry. A boy needs to be warned, perhaps more easily by dad than mom, that once he starts to grow up, his body begins to manufacture the sperms that will one day make it possible for him to be a father too. When the supply of sperms builds up to a certain level, the surplus are pushed down the erect penis and out of his body. This often happens at night, and the first he may know of it may be a wet patch on his pajamas when he wakes up. Whether accompanied by dreams or not, this can be vey disturbing for a boy who hasn't been told just what is going on.

GIRLS Children may know about the facts of life these days, but there are still some very funny stories going round the playground. A girl who has not been warned in advance by her mom could have a serious shock, or imagine that something has gone badly wrong, when her first period starts. Her mother may want to give her a scientific explanation. An egg from the ovary is released each month and, unless it has been fertilized, the spongy lining of the uterus and the special blood supply prepared to nourish it are not needed. So blood and mucus are passed out of the body every month.

Explanations apart, the main facts to make clear are:

- Monthly periods are normal, a sign that she is growing up naturally
- Periods may not be regular at first, so it's worth keeping a note of dates
- During periods she need not behave like an invalid but can carry on as normal

Advise her to change pads or tampons frequently to keep fresh and comfortable, and reassure her that it's perfectly all right to have a bath or shower, to wash her hair and take her usual quota of exercise. If there are repeated painful periods, it's best to consult your doctor. But don't suggest beforehand that there is likely to be undue pain or discomfort.

BOYS AND GIRLS

As well as being adequately prepared for the changes in their own bodies, it's useful if both boys and girls know what their opposite sex is going through! By telling boys about girls' periods and girls about boys starting to shave, their voices breaking and so on, you can—hopefully—help them to avoid suffering too much unwelcome teasing or embarrassment.

Both boys and girls need reminding of the need to wash often, especially in the places (under arms and between legs) where they are likely to sweat. The family can of deodorant spray could be pointed out as available for their use.

SEX

This three-lettered word often causes parents a lot of problems and embarrassment with their teenage children. Some find it much easier to talk about than others, but whatever your feelings there will be certain information you are passing on to your child whether you say anything about sex or not. By far the most important lessons he has on sex and marriage he will learn from watching how *you* relate to each other: how loving, caring and loyal you are, how much you enjoy talking, laughing, even arguing, but just being together. Your marriage is the biggest object lesson he'll ever have of what marriage is all about.

EXPLAINING SEX

Many parents feel quite unable to discuss sex facts with their own children. If you can't chat easily and informally, it is probably better to give him a book with the facts clearly explained and say you feel happier to do it that way. In spite of sex education at school, you have a responsibility to make sure he's not ignorant in this area. He also needs to be aware of the facts and controversies surrounding abortion, contraception and venereal disease (VD).

What may concern you most is the difference between your values and those of friends, magazines, television plays, books and teachers. Your values are what *you value* and it's important that you get these across in the course of conversation and discussion.

THE VALUE OF SEX

Many people these days think good reasons for having sex include the fact that:

- everybody else does
- it's enjoyable
- my boy-friend expects it
- the other boys will think me soft if I don't
- we love each other

The Bible takes a quite different line. The sex act makes two people one. It is an act of complete giving to another person which binds the two together in a bond of shared commitment. The law of the land recognizes this permanent relationship legally by marriage. Christians abide by this, but also see their relationship as a binding agreement made before God. Christians, in fact, value sex more highly than to use it as common currency or separate it from total involvement with one other person.

This way of thinking is as hard for young people to accept today as it was when the apostle Paul wrote his letters to young Christians living in a society with very loose sex morals. But God's plan is for the full and proper enjoyment of sex, protected from the emotional suffering and pain that society's misuse so often brings in its wake.

THE VALUE OF THE BODY

Christians believe that the whole of them belongs to God and that their bodies should be treated with respect. Not only does casual sex break God's law, but it brings the risk of disease to the individual and his unborn children. The incidence of VD has increased rapidly, partly because young people think it can be as easily cured as a cold. But sexually-transmitted diseases are never to be taken lightly.

THE VALUE OF LIFE

Because Christians value life, abortion can never be treated casually either. Opinions will vary as to what medical conditions make it necessary, but responsible action within marriage to prevent unwanted conception is part of Christian love, and teenagers should learn this.

FACTS FOR PARENTS

There are some facts of life which parents need to learn too. First of all, it may take a bit of a struggle to recognize that your son or daughter is a sexually mature person, with sexual feelings and desires. It *does* matter that parents should accept the fact, for unless they do, their reactions to boy- or girl-friends, and to the idea of marriage itself, can be unwelcoming and aggressive.

Masturbation is a natural way for young people to cope with their strong physical needs at a time when they are not ready for proper sex and marriage. Most people nowadays would accept that it is harmless provided that:

- it does not become obsessive
- it is merely a stage, not an end in itself
- it does not leave the teenager with too great a sense of guilt

Young people often find it hard to accept their own strong sexual feelings without a sense of guilt, and need reassurance that they are normal, that God accepts them and that his understanding help is available to them.

'Same sex' feelings It would be misleading to talk about homosexual feelings when describing this normal part of a boy's or girl's development. It is quite common to have a crush on someone of the same sex before going on to the stage of falling in love with one of the opposite sex. What is important is that it is recognized as part of growing up and that no one should encourage them to remain at this stage or imagine they are true homosexuals. This is one very important reason why young people should be protected from the attempts of 'gay' groups who wish to normalize homosexual tendencies and lower the age at which young people attend their clubs.

PATTERN TO FOLLOW
These stages in the development towards fully adult sexual relationships can be outgrown naturally provided there is a good pattern of happy married life for the teenager to imitate. But you may be a single parent or unhappily married. There will still be good models among relatives or in the church fellowship. If it's possible, talk about your own experiences honestly, especially as your children grow older, emphasizing what was good and positive. It is possible to give a fair assessment of the difficulties and an ideal to aim at, even though we are conscious of our own failures.

PREVENTIVE ACTION
Some mothers whisper darkly to daughters about the dangers of 'getting into trouble', while dads warn sons to 'treat your girl-

friend properly'. How much better to teach them consistently and clearly:

- the difference between right and wrong
- to think of the other person—not just take for themselves
- to be loyal, honest and responsible in personal relationships

You have been doing this since the year dot? All the more reason for believing that they will naturally carry over into their sexual relationships the lessons learned up to now in every other kind of relationship.

You can also use your veto to give some protection, without making it a vote of no confidence. Sheila's mom and dad talked it over and decided to say 'No' when she asked to spend the week with her boy-friend Dave. And Sheila wasn't surprised!

FURTHER INFORMATION

'An Adolescent in Your Home', US Printing Office, Washington, DC 20402
'Very Personally Yours', The Life Cycle Center, Kimberly-Clark Corp.,
    PO Box 9474, St. Paul, Minn. 55194. (Explains menstruation to a
    pre-adolescent.)
'The Miracle of You', Kimberly-Clark (For young adolescent girls.
    Explains menstruation, male and female reproductive systems, birth
    and hygiene.)
'Your New Self-Discovery', Kimberly-Clark (For older girls. Includes options
    for birth control.)
'Tell It Like It Is', Kimberly-Clark (Clearly explains the use of tampons.)

EDUCATION

One factor in your child's life that goes strictly by chronological age is the pattern of education laid down by the powers that be.

Before World War II, elementary school was defined as grades K-8, and many students did not go on to high school, usually located in the larger villages. Lack of transportation kept them from attending.

More recently, elementary schools, where a student has one core teacher, end at sixth grade. These schools are usually small and not too far away from a child's home. In some areas, a middle school, which covers grades 4-8, will combine a number of neighborhood schools. But more common is the junior high school (grades 7-8 or 9) which takes in students from many smaller elementary schools. The high school (grades 9 or 10-12) may be in the same building or it may be a separate structure.

CHOICE OF SCHOOL

CAN YOU CHOOSE?

All parents have the choice of opting out of the state system of education if they believe that it will benefit their child. But it is important to weigh the advantages of a private school very carefully. If the education and the facilities are to be anywhere near as good as in a state school, fees must be high. (There may be 'extras' to pay for and uniforms can be expensive.) Many parents feel that the cost is well worthwhile, but it needs careful thought and budgeting beforehand.

If you move from one school district to another in the middle of a school year and want your child to finish the term at his old school, many districts will give their permission, assuming you take care of the transportation. Many times schools charge tuition for students who do not live in their geographic area.

PAROCHIAL SCHOOLS

These are church (Protestant or Catholic) sponsored schools, which means the church authorities contribute part of the cost. They can, therefore, set the curriculum which will include religious training.

In some states the school district must provide transportation to students attending private schools within a set mileage limit from their home. Some of these schools have room and boarding facilities.

THE SCHOOL YOU FANCY

Whatever your choice, don't forget to consult the person most affected. Your child might much rather go to the same school as all his mates. Even a bright child can lose interest and his work can suffer if he's lonely or unhappy, however good the school may be. If your child wants to go to a public school and you feel strongly that he should attend a parochial school, talk the matter out and clearly list your reasons. In such large matters it is best not to force his hand.

CHRISTIAN WORSHIP AND INSTRUCTION IN SCHOOL

The federal government prohibits prayers and religious instruction in public schools during the school day. Teachers may teach about religions—Christianity as well as Mormonism, Judaism, and so forth—using them as literature, historical background, and cultural examples. But in no way is a teacher to influence the students for or against a particular religion.

Whatever your view may be as to the value of keeping prayer on the timetable by law, you will no doubt agree that in our present society it just isn't reasonable to expect your child to gain his Christian teaching during school time. The whole public school approach is likely to be from an agnostic, humanist viewpoint—a fact that parents need to realize.

The interpretation of the laws prohibiting prayer and religion in school varies from district to district. Some schools go so far as to call their Christmas concert a winter concert and yet others openly talk of Christian standards and heritage.

As we have discussed, some parents opt for enrolling their children in church-sponsored schools. Others feel that the quality of their family life and church programs adequately counter the teaching and peer pressure their children are hit with at school.

DECISIONS

WHAT'S YOUR LINE?

In most junior highs all the students take the same basic courses —math, science, English, and social sciences—with additional mini-courses in health, music, art, shop, and homemaking. Some more capable students may start foreign languages, algebra, and earth science.

Some time during junior high, your child, with guidance from you and the school staff, will make decisions which will affect his later life.

Will he take science, math, and foreign language courses,

usually considered the college prep course? Will he take business courses—record-keeping, shorthand, keyboarding—with a goal of seeking employment right after graduation? Will she take homemaking courses? Industrial arts, with an eye on an apprenticeship? Art courses to develop a talent?

Another option your child will have is the vocational/technical school in your area. Training in fields such as cosmetology, practical nursing, building trades, agriculture are open to tenth, eleventh, and twelfth graders. In such a program your child may attend a vocational school in another town or may attend the local high school part of the day and then be bussed to the voc school the other half. This is an inexpensive way to get special training.

Any high school student will have certain requirements to meet, but these are legislated on the state level. Most require three or four years of English, at least one year of math and science, four years of physical education, and a semester of health. Sixteen to twenty credits are required depending on the course requirements for the diploma.

Because the school realizes the importance of the choices set before the students, teachers, parents and pupil usually consult together about the whole matter. Schools vary, but you may get:

- a document sent home, outlining choices to be made
- a report on your child, giving some idea of his weak and strong points
- an invitation to a careers evening for parents and pupils which will give guidance on subjects needed for occupations he may want to follow
- an invitation to a parents' conference where teachers and guidance staff will be ready to discuss the case of your own child

It's vital that you get in on all this decision-making, as it is important for your child's future. When they advise you, teachers will take into consideration not only your child's aptitudes and preferences, but also:

- the need for some subjects that are basic to every walk of life to be compulsory: he won't usually be allowed to drop English or math and some schools also insist on one science subject being retained

- the importance of keeping education as wide and broad as possible at this stage: he will be discouraged from being too narrow or specialist in his choices
- the possibility that he will change his mind about what he wants to do: he will be encouraged to keep on any subject which might prove useful later on

EXAMINATIONS

Many states have standardized course requirements which lead to a competency examination at the end of the course.

To standardize this across the country, two examinations are given to eleventh and twelfth graders to assist colleges in determining the competency of the applicants. Some colleges require one test in particular but the majority of the schools will accept either. Many students take both sets:

SCHOLASTIC APTITUDE TEST

Offered seven times a school year at area testing centers on Saturday mornings. The three-hour test asks questions in math and English. A student takes it in May or June of his junior year so if he is not satisfied with his score he can retake it the following fall.

AMERICAN COLLEGE TEST

Offered five times a year on Saturdays, this tests in English, social sciences, math, and science.

HOME AND SCHOOL

One mother said, 'As soon as my children go through those school gates, I feel I lose them completely. They're not mine any more, and they're not mine until they come out again.' Not all parents cut off home and school so thoroughly. Some go to the other extreme and cannot leave their child well alone but are for ever up at the school fussing about his progress. Something in between is more helpful. Quite often teenage children are extraordinarily silent about what happens at school, so it can be a delicate matter finding out. But it's good for parents to have some idea of what goes on, as well as what is expected of their child, so that they can give the support needed at home.

BE PREPARED!

When a child leaves the neighborhood school and starts classes at the larger consolidated school, he will no doubt be unsettled for several months. The transition from junior high into high school, even if the student must again change schools, is not likely to be as traumatic as this first major change from elementary school into junior high.

Some helpful hints so your child is prepared:

- If the school's orientation session has not reduced your child's anxiety, take him on a tour of the building before opening day
- Make sure he labels books and supplies with his name and homeroom number
- Make sure he can use a locker combination
- See that he has the necessary supplies—some teachers ask for notebooks, others for folders
- Make sure he is aware of the importance of getting to classes on time and of asking questions when he doesn't understand
- If your child misses school, make sure he makes up missed work
- Provide child with assignment notebook and check periodically to see if he is completing homework

STARTING JUNIOR HIGH

This can be a daunting experience because an eleven- or twelve-year-old is usually not prepared to leave the neighborhood school. Some changes to be expected concern:

- Building: large and strange—a worry since pupils now move around to teachers' rooms
- Numbers: sheer size can be overwhelming—perhaps 1,000 or more instead of 200
- Friends: he may not know anyone in some of his classes
- Teachers: their approach will be different—many will let seventh graders realize they can't be spoon-fed any longer!
- Homework: he will probably have more but if he has a number of study halls, he may get it done in school
- Additional help: he may not be able to see the teacher at any other time than during class; free times do not coincide
- Status: he's been top of the elementary school—now he's bottom of the pile

There are various ways in which your attitude and general reassurance will smooth this time of transition and adjustment. 'Of course it seems strange at first, but you'll soon get used to it.' Make sure that you back up the school—at least in his hearing! Criticism from you won't give him confidence in this strange new system. Don't expect immediate results; allow for a settling-in period as he gets used to the new environment. And try not to be over-anxious. One educationist says: 'Children may suffer as much from anxious over-encouragement as from under-encouragement'—with which, as a teacher, I'd agree.

MAKING CONTACT WITH SCHOOL

After the more free and easy attitude towards parents at many elementary schools, you may feel that parents of junior and senior high children are expected to keep out. But you will probably have invitations to attend some or all of the following:

- Parents' and pupils' evening for new children before the fall term begins
- Open house in the fall term
- Open Day/Sports Day/Concert/Annual fair or fete
- American Education Week

Take every opportunity to go to the school and meet staff, but remember that one of these social occasions may not be the most convenient time to discuss your worries. So use the opportunity to mention that you'd like an appointment.

When you get your invitation to attend, your son or daughter may well say, 'Don't bother to go' or 'It's not important for you to be there' or even 'No one else's parents are going'. It's best not to take such hints seriously. Your child may have reached the normal stage of feeling embarrassed about the fact that he owns parents at all and would rather keep you in the dark. But if the school has invited you, they obviously think it worth your going. But be tactful and don't bounce up to your sheepish offspring in the corridor when he was hoping to sneak quietly past. Take your cue from him.

PARENT TEACHER ASSOCIATIONS

PTAs vary a good bit in their scope. Some are just fund-raising

organizations while others work alongside staff in helping the
school in many useful ways such as chaperoning or assisting
with uniforms. (These all-school groups tend to lose momentum
in junior and senior high, if they exist at all. But there will be
parent groups of special interest activities, such as band-boosters
or sports-boosters.) If you are both working and have little time
to spare for such help, try not to overlook notes that come
home requiring contributions to some activity in which your
child is involved.

HOMEWORK

They've worked all day—shouldn't they be free to play or relax
once they get home? There *should* be time for both, as well as
homework, at least in the early years. But homework serves a
useful purpose in showing how a pupil can tackle work without
teacher support or the school environment.

Here are some suggested ways in which parents can help:

● See that he sets aside the right amount of time before he's too
tired
● Find out how long work is supposed to take and check that he
neither does it too quickly nor takes too long over it. (If work in a
particular subject is regularly taking far too long, compare notes first
with a few other parents, then write to the member of staff.)
● Don't do the work for him but let him talk it over with you if it helps
him
● Go to school, if invited, to be told how some subjects (e.g. math)
are taught now
● 'Hear' his learning work for him: it's surprising what new information
you pick up and it can make it stick for him
● Try to provide somewhere for him to work away from too much
other noise and disturbance: a small folding table in a bedroom
might help, or even something flat to write on in a corner of the hall
or landing
● Have him do hardest assignment first
● Encourage him and don't compare him to siblings or children of
friends

EXAMS!

As years pass, the time spent in his homework cubby-hole will
get longer. Try to see that he gets a break before settling for the
night. A bit of television, or a family game plus a milky drink,
should help him sleep, and break the vicious circle of school,
work, bed, school.

You may have the opposite problem of trying to keep the reluctant scholar at his books. But as finals approach, most teenagers settle to work hard. On the whole they have to find their own best study routine and you can probably help most by providing a relaxed atmosphere, allowing for any added irritability on their part and encouraging them to go off to exams calmly, prepared to read the questions carefully and slowly and to give the answers they are asked for. Don't forget to make it clear that you expect neither a hopeless failure nor a budding Einstein/Shakespeare, and that you don't mind if he does better or worse than the boy next door/his sister/you both did.

'WHEN WE WERE APES?'

Whatever the subject—science, English literature, history—the likelihood is that your child will be taught it from the humanist point of view. This means that man, not God, will be seen as the center of everything and the one who can bring about the salvation of the human race. It will generally be taken for granted that man evolved by chance and is no more than a high form of animal life. Radio and television programs, books and magazines often make the same assumptions. Don't despair, but do be aware that your children are absorbing these views. The influence of the home is still very strong. But it is important that there is positive and wholesome Christian teaching in the family. That *doesn't* mean shoving your views down their throats, but being ready to discuss freely and answer their questions. Look together at what the Bible has to say about everything that concerns them and their world.

EXTRA ACTIVITIES

In many schools, as much student time and effort goes into extra-curricular activities as in studies.

Sports, band, chorus, orchestra, dramatics, school newspaper, and yearbook are just a few of the 'extras' tempting the student.

In a small high school, a student may be involved in two or three of these, which teach him leadership responsibilities, sportsmanship, self-confidence, and poise.

As a parent, you must assist your teen in deciding how many 'extras' he can take on and still maintain his health, studies, and Christian involvements.

You may find coaches, editors, directors, and band leaders controlling your child's life during after-school hours as well as on weekends, even during vacations. There may be no time for family, church, or for the teenager to relax.

Many teachers say that it is good for students to be involved in some activity apart from his studies and work, but overdoing it is another story.

CHRISTIAN ASSOCIATIONS

It will be a great help to a teenager if he can join up with Christians who attend his school. Youth for Christ (PO Box

419, Wheaton, Ill. 60189) sponsors junior and senior high Campus Life Clubs in homes, churches, or schools, depending on the local facilities and attitudes. Young Life (PO Box 520, Colorado Springs, Colo. 80901) sponsors weekly Young Life Clubs in homes. These clubs are primarily concerned with outreach or evangelism and feature skits, songs, and a Christian message. They sponsor smaller Campaigner Clubs for committed Christians concerned with Bible study and spiritual growth.

Both organizations have camping programs.

Most churches are concerned with their young people and sponsor their own youth programs.

FURTHER INFORMATION

'How to Help Your Children Achieve in School', US Printing Office, Washington, DC 20402

BEING A TEENAGER: WHAT'S IT ALL ABOUT?

Perhaps you once believed that the teenage cult was thought up by those who want to make a fast buck out of susceptible young people. Now you are going through some of the problems of a teenage son or daughter in your home. What *is* at the bottom of it all?

LIKE THE MEASLES
The fact that *you* may be going through a rough time is not helped by the fact that friends or relatives with children the

same age seem to be having no trouble at all. Before you start saying, 'Why can't you be like your cousin Sarah?', remember:

TEENAGE UNREST
- some get it badly—some get only a slight attack
- some get it at 11—others at 17—or any age between
- nearly all get a dose at some stage or other

A quiet, polite, well-turned-out teenager could in fact be the *real* worry. This difficult stage is quite normal—and it won't last for ever, as thousands of satisfied parents can testify!

The body changes of puberty take place because hormones —those special messengers the glands send out—become active. Until the hormone balance is achieved, there can be upsets in feelings and moods. A child is left feeling unlike his usual self and not knowing quite *what* he wants. At such times, he usually makes himself unpleasant in the family too. Perhaps girls are more likely than boys to go through these mood upsets. All women have to get used to certain mood changes during the monthly cycle, but it takes a bit of experience to cope. Boys often react by showing more aggression than usual during this stage.

HALF-WAY HOUSE
Growing up means being neither one thing nor another for a while. Some people—very gratifyingly—treat him as an adult, whereas others, probably including his parents, behave as if he's still a ten-year-old. He himself feels more grown-up at some times and in some ways than others. This can be frustrating and confusing. He knows deep down that he's not yet ready to cope with life but in other ways expects to be treated as adult. All this can make for arguments, tears, irritation and a feeling of insecurity—for parents as well as teenager.

DEPRESSION
Although there are severe cases of adolescent depression that need medical attention, remember that it is fairly normal for young people to be down in the depths at times. If you are really worried do not hesitate to ask for your doctor's advice, for teenage suicide is on the rise and not to be taken lightly.

Patience on the part of parents backed up by love and a sense of security will usually tide a teenager over his depression.

BEING HIMSELF

Up to now, your child may have been happy to go along as part of the family. Now he is reaching the stage when he wants to be himself, not just someone's son or brother. He's not content to be just an addition to dad and mom. Finding out who he is and learning to live with himself and his own views on life is going to take up a good bit of his time and thinking for the next few years. It's not an easy time for *him*. You aren't the only ones finding the going rough. But if he didn't go through this process, if he stayed your obedient, quiet, agreeable and agreeing boy, he'd never grow up into the man you want him to be, with convictions, beliefs and a life of his own.

PERSONAL VIEWPOINT

'My dad says' may have changed at five to 'My teacher says', but until adolescence—and sometimes after it—children tend to accept a parent's-eye view of the world. They may have their own likes and dislikes, but the parents' philosophy is usually taken over without too much reasoning or rejection. Now they seem to be throwing overboard all your most cherished ideals and beliefs.

They may:

- come up with their own quite different philosophy of life, which may change again quite quickly
- pick up ideas and beliefs popular with friends
- make their parents' beliefs their own in a new and personal way

AGE OF IDEALS

Many young people have high ideals. They do not like compromise or dishonesty and set themselves, and everyone else, high standards. When they see so-called Christian parents caring mainly about a color television or the latest registration number for their car, they are angry and disillusioned. There is a yawning gap between the world that should be and the world they see around them.

HOW TO COPE

Realizing that you *have* to cope with this stage of family life is half the battle. It's no good sitting back trying to carry on with the same old pattern of attitudes and reactions that worked well enough in earlier years, blaming all the disharmony on the teenagers. Try to understand what's happening to your growing-up child and agree together about your joint policy. Bring God into it. Remember that God is a Father. Remember that Jesus Christ went through the experience of being a teenager.

Luke's Gospel describes just one telling incident that took place when Jesus was nearly thirteen, the age at which a Jewish boy was considered a man. His parents, Joseph and Mary, were returning from a festival in Jerusalem, and found that Jesus was not in the family party. Worried and annoyed, they retraced their steps and finally found him in the temple. He was discussing and asking questions of the resident teachers there. When Mary told him off for not staying in the family fold, Jesus made it quite clear that he had a deeper duty to his Father, God. Gently but firmly he asserted his independence. But he also went back with them to Nazareth and 'was obedient to them'. Not all teenagers combine necessary independence and duty to parents so wisely and well!

NOT TOO UNDERSTANDING!

'I know just how you feel' or 'I used to write poetry when I was your age' may sound an understanding response, but may irritate too. Teenagers want to feel that their experience of a sunset or of falling in love is new—not something that others, particularly parents, have experienced before them. So don't spoil things by understanding them too well. Don't throw cold water over their enthusiasm, either. Of course they will probably not confide their deepest feelings to you. This may seem hurtful, especially if you have been used to a small son or daughter who told all. They are having to learn to stand on their own, and emotional ties have also to be broken. Be thankful, not jealous, if they make a confidant of someone whose judgement you too can trust.

PLENTY OF BACK-UP

Without making a song and dance about it, you can still give your child the support he badly needs. He may feel he hasn't made out very well—in study, in sport, with friends or with the opposite sex. He needs your moral support. He needs to be aware from your whole attitude that you still believe in him and think him of worth.

Teasing the children has probably always been a family custom—especially by dad. Don't be surprised if now they take the huff or take it to heart. Use enough tact and kindness to see which areas you'd better keep off. Don't tease about size or appearance, about personal habits or new enthusiasms. Don't nag either.

FUSS, FUSS, FUSS!

Apart from the rules needed for hygiene and health, just how much should parents fuss about general looks and tidiness at this stage? It may be mom who objects to scruffy jeans, or dad who dislikes the living-room looking a dump. A lot will depend on your temperament and on how you were brought up yourself. It often seems as if the fussier you have been with them up to now, the more grubby and untidy your child will become for a while.

Parents had better face up to the fact that unless life is going to be pure misery for everyone, nagging about looks or behavior has got to be kept in check. A constant flow of: 'Don't talk with your mouth full', 'Go and scrub your neck', 'Don't answer your mother back', 'Clear that junk out of your room', isn't going to make for family comfort or happiness. Parents need to talk things over together and plan joint action. Decide:

- the things that **really** matter: go to town on these, letting other points go
- how many warnings you will give before taking action
- what action you will take

You may decide that how he dresses is only important if he wants to go out with you. Provided a certain cleanness and tidiness is achieved to go to the football match with dad or the shops with mom, he or she can dress as they like to go out with friends. Provided bits and pieces are kept on a tray, models can be made in the living-room. If the bedroom is cleared ready for a weekly clean, it can be junky the rest of the time. 'Penalties' can be fitted to 'crimes'. If past copies of magazines aren't tidied on the cleaning day (after a reminder has been given), they are liable to be thrown out. Parents will have their own views on how to put these general guide-lines into action.

Now look again at the three 'musts' of love, discipline and independence and how they fit in with the difficult stage of growing up.

HOW MUCH LOVE?

This is not an age to kiss and cuddle or even to say 'I do love you!' But 'love', in the Bible sense of the word, is the very quality most needed at this stage. The famous Bible chapter about love is 1 Corinthians 13. Love is described there in terms of how it acts or behaves. Look at these keys to loving quoted from that chapter.

'LOVE IS PATIENT'
It *is* hard to keep your cool when a teenager's demands or actions are outrageous. Jackie's dad sees red whenever she arrives late for breakfast—which is most mornings—so days usually begin with a blazing row. Being patient does *not* mean putting up with inconsiderate or bad behavior time after time, but it does mean holding yourself in check (you're the mature one, remember) and looking for a better way of tackling the situation. Because:

'LOVE LOOKS FOR A WAY OF BEING CONSTRUCTIVE'
Mike has brought a note home from school complaining about the way that his math homework is being done—or not done! His mom tries to think how to find a quiet space for him to do homework. The television is on in the living-room and his two younger sisters play there too, so perhaps she can clear him a space at the kitchen table. His dad decides to make the effort to turn up at the school for that talk to parents on teaching

modern math. He might pick up enough to give him an idea of how to help Mike.

'LOVE IS NOT JEALOUS'

Sonia's mom finds it hard letting Sonia go out and enjoy herself while she sticks at home. It's not been easy for her to bring up two children on her own and she still feels young enough to get dressed up and go out herself, if she had the chance. She tries not to spoil Sonia's outing by a sting-in-the-tail remark as she leaves. 'Have a nice time, dear', not, 'You can expect to see me still stuck at this ironing-board when you get back'.

'LOVE IS NOT CONCEITED'

Parents have experience on their side, as they often remind their children, but do you honestly think you know the lot? 'If *we* had more say at church,' Geoff began, but his dad cut in with, 'What do youngsters like you know about running anything? You're scarcely out of diapers!' Love is humble enough to learn as well as instruct. Young people have worthwhile viewpoints to offer. At least be humble enough to listen to them because:

'LOVE IS NOT ILL-MANNERED'

Good manners often get quite forgotten in the family—between husband and wife as well as between parents and children. Perhaps your teenager *is* abominably rude to you, but give him a lesson in courtesy by being well-mannered to him. Good manners involve thinking how the other person feels, making him feel comfortable, not hurting him. With a teenager this could include:

- not going through his cupboards or notebooks or reading his letters
- not brushing aside his views but listening to him as you would to anyone else
- not making personal remarks about him or his friends
- not discussing him and his faults with your friends
- treating him with respect rather than contempt, despair, or disgust

'LOVE DOES NOT KEEP A RECORD OF WRONGS'

'That's the third time this week you've left your bike out.' 'I haven't forgotten how you behaved at Easter.' 'If I've told you once I've told you a hundred times . . .' All true, no doubt, but harking back to previous crimes which were dealt with at the time is neither helpful nor loving. It doesn't help a teenager to imagine that parents are keeping a score card of his mistakes. What a wonderful thing it is that God forgives us so completely that he blots out the past! That's the extent of his love. He lets us start again with a new sheet.

'LOVE NEVER GIVES UP'

God loves us, and he believes in us. It's a wonderful encouragement to success to know that he looks at us and sees the people he can make of us one day, if we'll let him. Rightly or wrongly, a lot of teenagers get the impression that their parents have given them up as a bad job. Love has faith in the person loved. Some parents may be genuinely afraid that the child they knew and loved has disappeared for ever, leaving a reckless and uncongenial stranger in his place. He *will* emerge, not as the child they once knew and loved, but as an adult with all the endearing qualities of the child and the added individuality and independence of an adult.

Parents must 'believe all things'. The teenager himself is perplexed at his own new emotions and reactions. Parents who don't give up on him but go on believing in his worth make it that much easier for him to emerge into adulthood with certainty and with their relationship unharmed by the scuffles and quarrels of adolescence.

FREEDOM—HOW MUCH?

'Can I watch the late-night movie?'
'Can I go to the dance with June?'
'Can I go to Montreal with the French class at school?'
'Can we go camping next weekend?'

Here are a few points worth taking into consideration when deciding on what permission to give:

- **Agree together:** if one isn't happy about the project, it may mean both deciding against. But sort it out in private and stick to your decision together.
- **Consider expense:** is the trip to Canada warranted at this stage? Would you afford it better later and would he benefit from it more when older?
- **The rest of the family:** how is his bid for freedom going to spoil the fun or the chances of the rest of the family?
- **Health:** will late nights, or whatever else is involved, harm his health?

From this age on, youngsters are likely to trot out the 'I'm the only one in the class who isn't allowed to . . .' line of talk. Take it with a pinch of salt. I once got a whole class of girls to admit that they all said that at home!

GIVING MORE ROPE

Of course you will gradually be extending the scope you give your child for doing things alone or with friends. One bit of freedom responsibly used encourages you to give more. But a child growing up still feels a good deal safer with parents who put limits on what he asks to do. One bit of him may be thankful for the excuse of not having to do something that he's still a little unsure of being able to cope with. Parents who say 'No' provide a useful way out—whatever his outward reaction. He can always complain to his friends about fussy parents, although he is secretly relieved. Parents walk a tightrope between giving too much freedom too soon and keeping their child tied to their apron-strings.

SAFETY FIRST

When he was tiny, you had to decide whether it was safe to let him go alone to the corner shop or play on the swings. You tried to steer the right course between the extremes of wrapping him in cotton wool and exposing him to risk of real danger. Do the same now. Remember that now, as then, giving sufficient guidance and information is important. For example, when he was tiny you taught him how to cross roads and warned of the dangers of carelessness. Now you will teach him about the effects of alcohol and warn him of the dangers of drinking too much or driving too fast.

ON CONDITION

Parents have every right to give *conditional* permission to certain requests. Your son or daughter wants:

- **to stay out late and return home alone:** you will want to know **where** she is to be all evening. I sometimes used to ask for an emergency phone number, just as I gave them one when I went out.
- **to go off with friends in the car belonging to one of the group:** it is wise to check on fitness of car, driver **and** number of passengers to be transported before agreeing to that jaunt.
- **to have a motor bike:** if he's saved up or earned enough to buy a motor bike, check that he's well aware of road safety rules and insurance legislation, has adequate training and protective clothing.

THE ANSWER IS 'NO'

Sometimes you have to put your foot down and it's not pleasant. There may be storms or tears or pleas, but if together you've made your decision on safety grounds, stick to your guns. All-night parties, certain night spots or other activities you may feel you should ban for at least a few more years, even at the risk of being called old-fashioned or hard-hearted.

GOOD COMPANY

You may be worried not so much about your child's physical danger as his moral danger. He may have got in with a crowd who think it clever to go drinking, smash up property or indulge in football hooliganism. Or your daughter may have palled up with a couple of girls who go out with the purpose of picking up fellows.

It's much more difficult to put your foot down in these cases, and it's important to do so in a way that causes the least amount of loss of face for them. But you are bound to protect your children from dangers they are not ready to withstand.

Spiritual dangers from friends without your moral standards, or from teachers or books that are blatantly anti-Christian pose an even trickier problem. You may also need to warn your teenager about the danger of dabbling with the occult. Young people often play with a ouija board in school lunch-hours or use other methods of getting answers from the spirit world. Not all spiritism is hocus-pocus. Too many have found themselves ending up as frightened victims of forces they themselves set in action.

BE POSITIVE

In the physical world you can't stop a child from coming into contact with dirt or harmful germs. If you tried to over-protect him he would have no natural resistance to them. But you do disinfect where necessary and provide the right kind of healthy regime to give him a good chance against infection.

It's the same with spiritual dangers. Over-protection would be counter-productive; but it's not possible anyway to make him avoid all possible sources of infection. Provide the right kind of wholesome diet of good books and discussion, and use the disinfectant power of prayer. Praying for growing children is not an airy-fairy bit of advice, but a practical and important factor in maintaining their spiritual health and bringing them safely through the hazards of growing up.

KEEPING THEIR BALANCE

Being mature includes having a balanced outlook on life. To teenagers, the idea of balance is usually dull and unadventurous. They do nothing by halves. The latest craze or leisure activity absorbs all waking thoughts. You'll be waging a losing battle if you try to ban a cult figure from conversation or tear down his picture from the bedroom wall, but you may have to limit the time spent watching sport, listening to records, or whatever the lastest craze may involve, if no time is left for anything else. Homework must be done as well as the usual jobs at home. So without too many jibes or total bans you have to insist that some sense of balance is maintained.

HOW TO DISCIPLINE

I remember the day when my older son, aged about eleven, picked me up bodily in a show of physical strength. I realized that my days of putting him, by brute force, in his room for punishment were certainly over. So what sanctions can be applied to strapping young men or dignified young women?

A MATTER OF COURSE

If you have always been firm and meant 'no' when you've said it, then long before this age your son or daughter will have accepted your authority without the backing of force. How you dealt with the toddler rebellion has a lot to do with how well you can cope with the teenage rebellion. Dictatorship is not likely to work and teenagers need to know that you do not exert your authority unless you believe it to be really necessary. When it *is* necessary, you try to keep to certain helpful ways of dealing with the situation.

Be understanding 'We quite see why you want to go there, but we feel we can't allow it for a year or two longer because there are too many risks attached', rather than, 'Why ever do you want to go to that dump? I suppose you think you can do what you like now, but you've got another think coming!'

Be reasonable Give honest reasons for what you forbid. They may not agree with your reasoning but can at least recognize that you are not just being difficult.

Be consistent It's only too easy to act according to how we feel. Parents who have had a bad day at the office may snap a refusal to a request they would allow on a sunnier day. Try to be as consistent as you were when they were tiny.

DON'T BE LEGALISTIC

It's a family, not a court of law. Don't stand at the front gate with a stop-watch, dad. A few minutes later than the appointed time doesn't *really* matter. If he is some time after the agreed hour, then you have every right to let him know how worried you've been and to insist he rings up if he's unavoidably delayed. If you aren't on the phone, he may only go out if he does keep to the agreed homecoming time.

BE FIRM

Older as well as young children prefer to know just where they stand. Constant nagging and unkept threats do little good and a lot of harm. If he is too long in the bathroom or persists in leaving it unfit for further use, then, without more than one or two warnings, he must be the last in the bathroom (if that is a practical possibility) or clean the bathroom at the weekend. Punishment does need to be seen as a reasonable consequence of the crime. Taking away his guitar because he's been playing too noisily or too often is childish. Working out a scheme of times at which he may practice is a reasonable way of sorting things out.

GET ROUND THE TABLE

In fact, that kind of sorting out is the best approach. Adjustment of his behavior to fit in with the needs of others rather than punishment for its own sake is the order of the day. You need not put him in the dock while you act as judge. Disciplining teenagers calls for discussion, reason, explanation and an agreed way of dealing with the troubled situation for the benefit of all.

FAMILY ROWS

Is this a subject you'd rather keep quiet about? You can't imagine others have the same troubles. But conflict is bound to occur when three or four adults are living under the same roof. Sometimes a row blows up because:

- rebellious teenager attacks your authority
- an accumulation of minor irritations spills over into anger and a real flare-up
- one or more of the family has had a difficult day at work and tempers held in check there quickly spill over at home

After a row, it's important to think about how it started and to relieve any guilty feelings others may have by explaining what led to the outburst.

Let's look at the alternatives to family rows and see if they offer a solution. There will *not* be family rows in the following situations:

- Where every member of the family is a saint: all will happily obey or give way and none will hurt or wrong another
- Where one member, perhaps dad or mom, is so dominating that the others give way by silent, mutual consent

● Where parents unite to indulge the small child, then later to placate the teenager, giving way to his whims and building family life around him

● Where angry members of the family smoulder in silence, or sulk, and no one speaks for a few days until the cloud lifts

● Where natural anger is pushed down and bitterness or resentment takes its place—and ulcers, rashes and other physical reactions follow in many cases

It seems, then, that except in the case of the family of saints (not yours?), the alternatives to showing anger are none too healthy either. Yet we still feel guilty about rows, perhaps because we fear the powerful emotion of anger (both in ourselves and others) and because we think it's unchristian to be angry.

A SAFETY VALVE?

The Bible has things to say about anger. Surprisingly, perhaps, it talks about God's anger. It shows us that Jesus Christ was sometimes angry when he was on earth. So anger is not always evil. But because our human emotions have all been poisoned by evil, anger, in our experience, very often *is* wrong. We can be angry about the wrong things, with the wrong person, at the wrong time, for the wrong reason (often out of wounded pride), with the wrong results.

But anger, like hunger, love or sexual desire, is a perfectly natural human feeling and we are bound to experience it, though we may have learned to stifle and suppress it. A better way is to learn to handle it safely. Family rows are never ideal, but properly controlled and limited they may provide a better safety valve than other outlets for dealing with conflict.

HOW TO HANDLE ANGER

In his letter to the Ephesians, the apostle Paul gives a guide to the best way to cope with anger: 'Be angry but do no sin; do not let the sun go down on your anger and give no opportunity to the devil.'

'Be angry' So the Bible doesn't tell us never to be angry. Anger can be the other side of the coin of love. Think of a few family situations where it would be positively wrong and *un*loving not to be angry:

- with a teenage daughter who broke rules by accepting a lift from a stranger after dark
- with a teenage son found bullying a much younger brother
- with a teenage son or daughter who arranged to go out with friends knowing grandma was coming for her birthday dinner

(Try thinking of some occasions where a teenage son or daughter might rightly feel angry with you!)

'Do not sin' Here's the condition for anger and it's not so easy to keep. We sin when we let anger lead to:

- saying quite unfair things about another person: 'You care about no one but yourself!'
- attacking someone where it really hurts: 'You always were the stupid one.'
- becoming violent: either attacking physically or screaming and becoming emotionally out of control
- dragging up the past: 'I'll never forget what you did to me when . . .'
- destroying another's self-respect: 'You aren't worth bothering with.'

No wonder we're scared of anger! It so easily gets out of control and the scars left by things done or said in a bad row may never completely heal. So with God's help we must not let anger lead on to what is wrong. Parents, as more mature people, should have more control over anger than the teenager. One psychiatrist suggests that parents do well to concentrate their anger on the action that has angered them, rather than the teenager who has committed it.

For example: 'I feel absolutely mad when I see this food spoiled—it cost a lot and took ages to prepare. I am not going to see that happen again so you can do something about turning up on time', instead of, 'You are a thoughtless, selfish child. You don't care about the hours I've slaved getting this food ready and you haven't the decency to come and get it on time. You never give a thought for anyone but yourself and your precious friends.'

'Don't let the sun go down on your anger.' In other words, don't go to bed angry. A new day needs a new start uncluttered by yesterday's failures. Besides, it gets much harder to say sorry after a night's sleep. Children brought up from the start on this policy by parents who practice it themselves, will take it for granted that matters are put right before everyone settles for the night. It need not be the same person who says sorry first—usually there's no one who doesn't need some forgiveness. It won't hurt dad to be the one to climb down first sometimes. A modern version of that verse says 'Don't be angry all day'. So if you have a breakfast row, it shouldn't smoulder till dinner-time. The message is that anger is only safe if it's quickly defused and quickly over.

AFTERMATH

Some families prefer not to wallow too much in apologies and you will find your own ways of getting reconciled. What really matters is that:

- no bitterness or resentment is left on anyone's part
- family atmosphere is really put right
- lessons have been learned: each side has seen the other's viewpoint and learned from it
- the relationships have grown as a result of the clash, not been stunted as they might if everyone had smouldered inwardly and smothered anger

HUSBAND AND WIFE ROWS

It is worth thinking whether children or teenagers should be allowed to witness rows between their parents. Remember that it's always more painful to witness a row than to take part in it. Children may witness the row but not be aware of the loving reconciliation that will follow. They may thus get a wrong impression of the relationship. However, children need to know that parents *do* have differences, and even rows, yet still love each other and have a secure marriage. So perhaps the answer is that differences of opinion may be witnessed but full-blooded rows should be kept private. And of course the same rules about handling anger apply here too.

FURTHER INFORMATION

'Parent-Teenager Communication: Bridging the Communication Gap', by Millard Bienvenu, Public Affairs Pamphlets

'Coming of Age: Problems of Teenagers', Paul H. Landis, Public Affairs Pamphlets

'Mental Health Is a Family Affair', Dallas Pratt and Jack Neher, Public Affairs Pamphlets

'What Can You Do About Quarreling?', Harry Milt, Public Affairs Pamphlets

HOME AND . . .

From the age of five or even earlier, life for your child became a matter of home and other places too. By the time he is twelve or thirteen, you may feel that the home part of the arrangement is low on the list. Yet even in his later teens home can still be somewhere secure and reliable, where known standards are recognized and followed. It can still be the place to provide refuge when the going gets tough, somewhere that makes sense of the other bits of life because of understanding and trustworthy parents.

HOME SWEET HOME

Doesn't always seem that way? A house full of near-adults brings its problems and crises. There are often particular trouble-spots. Squabbles or scenes occur time after time over the same matters, so it's worth sitting down and looking for a solution to save the wear and tear of too many tiresome action replays.

KITCHEN SINK DRAMA

Dad has a church committee meeting, John's doing homework and Katy is on the phone to a friend. So mom does the dishes single-handed once again. Or mom is at evening class and Pat and Keith wrangle so noisily about whose turn it is to do the dishes that dad turns them both out of the kitchen and does them himself before mom gets back. Doing the dishes is only one duty that could come on your agreed jobs schedule. You may want to pin something up on the memo board in the kitchen so that no one can dispute decisions afterwards. Remember that:

- stay-at-home housewife should not do all the out-of-hours chores
- boys can take equal shares and do the same jobs as girls
- timetable will need revising: older teenagers may have less weekday time for helping
- everyone should know how to operate any new piece of machinery (e.g. washing-machine)

CIRCUMSTANCES ALTER CASES?

Mrs James is a full-time housewife with an only daughter. She makes Joanne's bed, tidies and cleans her room and shoos her out of the kitchen telling her to enjoy herself while she can.

Mrs Roberts is a teacher who runs her home, with six children. All of them have their allotted tasks to do or else the whole system would grind to a halt.

Mrs Phillips has an elderly mother-in-law living nearby. On the days when she goes across to clean and cook for her, John and Julie expect to bring in any bits of shopping required.

How much your family helps may depend on how many of you there are and parents' working hours. While too heavy a load of work or responsibility is not good for a teenager, doing everything for them can be just as unkind. Children need to recognize that families function best when everyone contributes to their smooth running.

IN AN EMERGENCY

Any eleven-year-old should be able to:

- get a simple meal (e.g. bacon and eggs)
- make tea and coffee
- work the washing-machine
- know where to find cleaning things, food supplies
- shop sensibly
- change sheets
- sew on buttons
- iron simple articles
- answer phone or door politely and take a message accurately

By fifteen or so, a teenager should be able to hold the fort during several days' absence from home of the usual caterer and housekeeper.

TELEVISION SPECIAL

A few rough and ready rules may be needed to regulate viewing. Parents will retain the right to decide whether a program is suitable or not. This may be because it goes on late on a week-night or because you don't approve of the content. If you are in doubt, watch with them and then at least you can discuss the program afterwards. It is right to switch off if a program is morally harmful—for instance, if violence is glorified or sex is cheapened or perverted. But keeping your family's standards high means keeping them yourself. Constant viewing of tripe may do more harm than the occasional program which you find disconcerting but which has a serious message to give. Devise a scheme for dealing with constant rows over which program on which channel. Either make it a matter of taking turns or give priority to the program which can be proved to be more educational or worthy!

GETTING-UP TIME

This is another possible trouble-spot. Constant calls to get up or to get out of the bathroom can make mornings wearing. Teenagers who refuse to respond to repeated calls may learn most quickly by being left to be late for once. And don't forget that dad *is* still head of the family outfit and should have his proper place in the scheme of things. A good wife and mother sees that he gets due consideration just as a good husband makes sure that his wife is not reduced to tears too often by thoughtless or sharp-tongued teenagers.

GETTING ON WITH THE OTHERS

If you have an only child you have your own particular problems, but if you have several children you will have discovered some of the problems that arise from getting on together. Much depends on how many there are, their temperaments, and sex and age differences. Whatever their order in the family, each child can have his special advantages and disadvantages, in relation to the rest. Here's an example from a family of three:

- **Problems for oldest:** he's had to grow up more quickly and give a lead
- **Problems for youngest:** others have done everything before him; he's spoiled or squashed by older brothers or sisters
- **Problems for middle:** he has had no time at home as an 'only'; he lacks 'specialness' of first or last child

It is natural for brothers and sisters to quarrel. They are learning to share, to live with others and to realize that they have no right to the center of the stage. But as parents you want to avoid long-term resentments or long-term damage done to one child's personality by another. You can help by:

- treating **every** child as worthwhile and as an individual
- not making comparisons: 'He's the clever one' or 'She's the dunce'
- taking time with each one separately as well as together
- having no favorites
- keeping an eye open for undue bossing, teasing or too much dependence of one on another
- encouraging the particular gifts and aptitudes of each

If every member of the family knows that he is loved and valued by his parents for himself, he's not likely to suffer serious damage from brothers and sisters. They will all most probably be the best of friends by choice in the years ahead.

HOME AND CHURCH

'My thirteen-year-old doesn't want to come to church. Should I make him?' asks a worried mother. It may relieve her straight away to realize that there is nothing unusual about this. We've already noted that the teenager needs above everything to get away from following in his parents' footsteps and to become an individual in his own right. Very often he makes some 'demo' to prove his point—especially over any matter where he feels parents hold very strong views or tend to keep the apron-strings too tight.

MAKING HIS OWN CHOICES

When he is young, a child's parents decide for him, but as he gets older more and more of the choosing comes from him. You may rightly feel that it's still your job to override what could lead to danger or unhappiness. So how about going to church? Should *he* decide or *you*? At thirteen you might succeed in dragging him bodily to a service, but you can't command his response to God. You will need much tact and good sense to act rightly—and the right way could be different in different families or at different stages of development.

You may decide to encourage attendance at his usual youth activity at church and let him off going with you to services until things have cooled a bit. You might arrange a compromise: he comes with you every other Sunday or once a month. Try to keep it low key and loving as well as firm. You may gently insist on some kind of attendance while he is in your home, just as he abides by other family ways of behavior.

The important thing is not to let the very Christian values you cherish and want him to accept—love, joy, peace—go out of the window in some bitter and fruitless argument. You can't *make* him love God but you can give him some idea of what that love is like. Insist on your minimum requirements, then pray and play a waiting game.

WHAT DOES THE CHURCH OFFER?

That's the question we usually ask, rather than, 'What have I got to offer the church?' Belonging to a church is like belonging to a family: it involves giving and taking. Children need to learn from parents' own attitudes that belonging to a church is neither a weary slog nor a joy-ride. Have a look at your own involvement with your local church fellowship. It should provide you with the opportunity to:

- pray with others
- worship with others
- learn with others
- share with others
- provide for others' needs
- draw help from others

It sounds ideal, but let's hope your church provides enough of these activities to suit the whole family.

YOUTH GROUPS

You could contact your local church to find out if it runs a youth group. There are also many organizations, mostly attached to a local church, meeting the special needs of teenage boys and girls. They provide Christian instruction and run midweek activities of great variety to cover the interests of nearly anyone. Many run camps. Many churches have their own Girl Scout or Boy Scout groups. Some of the main organizations are listed at the end of the chapter. For further information, write to the addresses given, enclosing a stamped envelope for reply.

WHAT'S NEXT?

So far, you as parents may have been responsible for your children's Christian upbringing. This may have involved:

- Christian teaching: at home/church/school
- baptism or dedication as a baby
- examples of Christian living at home

Now that they are teenagers, you may want to see them take steps of Christian commitment for themselves, perhaps entering upon full church membership. This is obviously a decision each individual young person must take after careful thought and prayer. The conditions for entry will vary according to the church attended.

THEME AND VARIATIONS

There is so much variation, even in churches of the same denomination, that it's difficult to outline what practices each follow. The main difference is between churches that baptize a child as a baby and those that have a service of blessing or dedication at that stage and defer membership and baptism to a later age.

Those churches that practice infant baptism have a confirmation service at a later date, often at the adolescent stage, when the young man or woman can confirm the promises made on their behalf at baptism. Those churches that practice believer's baptism usually baptize by immersion. The person to be baptized confesses his faith in Christ and his determination to follow him, and is then put right under water, rather than being sprinkled with it. Many churches hold instruction classes to prepare young people for confirmation or baptism and church membership.

It is wrong if these important rites become no more than the thing to do at a certain age or stage, and parents need to guard against pushing teenagers into taking such an important and decisive step until they are ready.

Communion Many different churches and denominations now have an 'open table'. This means that they welcome to the communion all who love the Lord Jesus Christ, whether they belong to their church and have been through their particular ceremonies or not.

KEEP PRAYING!

It's easy enough to keep reminding parents that they should pray for their children, but just how should they set about it? In his New Testament letter, Peter writes about the importance of husband and wife keeping their relationship right so that their prayers will be effective. He seems to see joint prayer as an important factor in marriage. So it's ideal when both parents are Christians and can pray together for their children. This may not be possible—you may be bringing up your family single-handed. Why not arrange a regular meeting with other moms or dads who feel the same need to pray for their teenagers?

WHAT FOR?

Prayer is not like taking out an insurance policy against trouble, illness or failure. It isn't presenting to God a shopping list of things we'd like. Prayer helps us to understand God's view of things and to find out how he can help us to bring something good and valuable even out of the worst muddles or accidents. We *can* ask for our children:

- God's protection—against spiritual as well as moral and physical dangers
- that God's Spirit will go on speaking to them through their experiences
- that the home may be a place where children will find it **easy** to believe in God and see him at work

The Bible tells us that those who come to God must believe he exists and that he rewards those who come to him. What kind of rewards can you expect from your prayers?

- A changed attitude to circumstances: prayer changes **people** even more than things
- Wisdom to deal with your children in the best way (God promises wisdom to all who ask for it)

● The assurance that God's love surrounds your children and protects them
● The comfort of making requests to one who loves your children **more than you**

TWO OR THREE . . .

Jesus promised to be present when two or three met in his name. Some have seen in this a reference to a family of dad, mom and child. It's not easy to 'meet in his name' in the home as the children reach teenage years, but if the home is to have a focal Christian point, some kind of family worship is still needed. The length of time spent seems to me less important than the fact that outward recognition is given to Christ as the center of the home. Perhaps it could be grace before one meal in the day, offered not in some well-known formula but as a brief, personal prayer to meet the needs of the family for that day.

HOME AND AWAY

Shared memories are an important part of belonging to a family. It's natural that as children get older they will want to go out with friends of their own age and go to camps or vacations designed for young people. But there still is value in time spent together as a family—not as a dreary must, but as a deliberate choice some of the time. Such activities together could include:

● days out to somewhere of interest to everyone
● vacation for the family (our last family vacation was fixed when our eldest was 20 and the youngest 16)
● games played together: tennis, swimming, or badminton played on a small square of lawn
● indoor activities: a jumbo jigsaw or crossword, board games, paper and pencil games

HOMESICK?

Some children can go away from home without turning a hair, but many can suffer quite badly from homesickness. It helps him to know that it's a common reaction; and it's a good idea to give him a 'practice-run' by a stay overnight with a family friend or relative.

HOME AND LEISURE

Parents usually understand their teenager's need for leisure time and don't object when it is filled with worthwhile activity. But they do get anxious if a teenager seems to be wasting time just doing nothing or mooning around. In fact, doing nothing is a normal and often helpful occupation at this stage. There is a great deal to be thought about and dreamed about. The body and mind need catching-up time. So it's better not to try to organize him too conscientiously and not to worry if his idea of time off is lying on his bed listening to so-called music.

PARENTS NEED LEISURE TOO

At this stage of life, many couples have a tight schedule of duties at home, work and church as well as other responsibilities, often to elderly parents or relatives. There seem to be no evenings free to please yourselves. Yet it is specially important to maintain the habit of doing things together and to keep your own marriage fresh and interesting.

It's only too easy—you've seen it in other couples—to wake up to having nothing in common but the children and *they* have left home. So it's worth making real efforts to enjoy a shared interest. Go to a concert, the theatre or some kind of local group—for growing dahlias or digging up the past, just as your fancy takes you. It's important to *reserve* time to talk together, and to go on discovering each other, bodies and minds.

'Baby-sitters' can be a problem during early teen years. With children too old to be 'sat with', yet too young to be left alone after about 9 o'clock at night, parents have to use tact in inviting a relative or old friend to drop in for the last hour or more of their time out or else curtail late nights out by themselves for a year or two. This stage, like every other, passes quickly, and it's not long before your eighteen-year-old reproves *you* for being late home as you quietly sneak in at the front door.

SUNDAY, LOVELY SUNDAY
What's Sunday for?

- doing nothing?
- visiting family?
- pleasing yourself?

- household jobs?
- going to church?
- pleasing others?

The Bible teaches that Sunday *should* be a day of rest. Since a change is often as good as a rest, doing different things as well as doing nothing can be included. But Sunday is also a day to keep apart for God and for other people's needs. Many parents will have made their own pattern for Sundays which may include:

- worship of God
- meeting with other Christians
- learning about God
- resting
- helping in church activity

- seeing parents or family
- spending time as a family together
- using home for others (lonely, elderly)

Children may get to the stage of wanting to opt out of some of these once-shared activities. Parents will use their own discretion but will keep the right to set the pattern of Sunday which they have chosen for their home.

READ ANY GOOD BOOKS LATELY?
'My son's thirty now but he'd still enjoy "Archie" if he had the chance!' a lady told me. Certainly many adolescents read comics more than anything else. Reading these probably does little harm, provided the diet is balanced by including something more worthwhile and truer to life.

Keep some eye on the content of what your children read. Some romance may be harmless, but high schools are 'crawling' with occult novels. (They are all some kids will read.)

Look out for the interestingly written and well-produced books on your church bookstall to read for yourselves and to leave for the rest of the family to dip into. Lively and attractive Christian magazines such as *Campus Life* can be enjoyed by teens, others by the whole family. See that your son or daughter has a personal copy of a modern translation of the

Bible, such as the 'Good News Bible', and supply some Bible reading aids to suit the stage he's at.

HOME AND OTHERS

It's easy to parcel out time into so many hours for work, sleep, chores, necessary travel, leisure, even church-going, without thinking much about the needs of other people. It's good if young people learn through what goes on in their own family that 'it is more blessed to give than to receive'. Family outings may sometimes be stretched to include someone otherwise housebound and an invitation to Sunday dinner or tea extended to someone elderly, living alone, or a newcomer to the area.

Teenagers have a great record of care and service to others. Some of the youth organizations already listed run work camps and parties in order to help the handicapped or elderly.

COPING WITH FRIENDS

This is an age when friends are very important to a boy or girl. Instead of one special friend there may be a whole gang of them that go round together. It matters a lot to look the same and do the same as the others. Being accepted by his own age group is more important than being accepted by grown-ups. Many of the ways in which he behaves (talking, eating, dressing) will depend on how the rest behave. It's not going to help if you make scathing remarks about the less savory members of the gang when they come to call. Instant dislike by parents is usually guaranteed to make a friend seem more desirable anyway, and most young people will be loyal to the friends of their choosing.

PARENTS' FRIENDS

Parents have rights too in this matter of friends. Children often go through a stage of being downright rude to adult visitors to the home. Women friends of mom's may be special targets for their bad manners. If parents treat children's friends with courtesy, they have every right to insist at least on a pleasant greeting for their own friends. Happily, you may choose friends in common and know whole families with whom you have shared outings and holidays. Even these arrangements may not survive indefinitely though; this can certainly be an age of fixed likes and dislikes and very little tolerance.

FURTHER INFORMATION

'Campus Life' magazine, 465 Gundersen Dr., Carol Stream, Ill. 60187
Campus Life Books offer a line of Christian books for teens, including:
   'Do You Sometimes Feel Like a Nobody?' and 'The Trouble
   With Parents'

Interdenominational youth organizations:
Awana Youth Associates, 3201 Tollview Dr., Rolling Meadows, Ill. 60008
Christian Service Brigade, Box 150, Wheaton, Ill. 60187
Pioneer Clubs, Box 788, Wheaton, Ill. 60189
Word of Life, Schroon Lake, NY 12870

THE EVERYDAY BUSINESS OF LIVING

Getting meals, doing housework, cleaning, sewing and earning enough money to pay the bills seem to take up a good bit of living time at this stage of the family's life.

MONEY

It's not easy to budget: food bills may be large, adult-size clothes cost more and there seems no end to the things required for school and leisure, quite apart from normal running costs at home. You may think again about both being wage-earners if mom has been at home full-time up to now.

Don't forget that what you gain in money you will lose in time. A parent at home full-time can afford to listen to the family, without one eye on the clock. Building up relationships takes time, and knowing a family well doesn't happen automatically when no one has a minute for anything beyond getting the essentials done in the evenings and at week-ends.

Parents will make their own decision but it can be a mistake to see work outside the home as more interesting and stimulating than home-making. Now that the days of small children are past, it's possible to give time to creating interesting meals, or interesting clothes according to skill and inclination. Quite a bit of money can be saved by careful housekeeping, which is not possible when both parents are out all day. Older children *do* still need their mom and it's often a matter of being quietly and unselfishly available when required.

HELP WITH THE FINANCES

You are sure to complain about being hard up. But are you sure you are getting all the benefits in cash or facilities that you are entitled to? If your income is low, check with the social services department of your local government to see whether or not you qualify for aid. If you are widowed, check with your Social Security office. If you have a handicapped child you might be eligible for some Medicard benefits. If in doubt, ask. The government's benefits are for everyone who qualifies—not just for the other guy.

ALLOWANCE

How much allowance you give will depend on:

- how much you can afford
- how much it's good for your teenager to have
- what you expect him to use it for

Allowance is usually understood as money to spend on extras such as sweets, for saving towards a coveted possession, or for using for gifts to others. As a child grows older, it might increase along with the teen being responsible for more of his own care, such as bus fares, some clothing, recreation.

Some parents think children should learn to manage

money in this way before leaving school, though if they plan to begin earning at sixteen, you may think that is time enough to begin. If he is likely to be dependent on you and a government grant for a number of years as a student, it is better preparation to learn how to budget for main needs (clothes, fares, entertainment, giving) before college days begin.

Your teenager's attitude to money will be colored by yours. If you have taught and practiced giving generously to God and to others, he is likely to follow suit. Suggest that he keeps an account book and makes a note of expenses so that he can see where the money goes. It will also give him a leg to stand on if he has to convince you that he needs an increase. It's probably better to give too small an allowance than too large a one at first. Spoiling him with too much money can lead to foolish and extravagant spending, and give a false idea of what his position will be like when he becomes a wage-earner.

BY THE SWEAT OF HIS BROW?

Perhaps he's mad to get an electric guitar, or she wants skates. They suggest getting an out-of-school job to earn some money. Provided it won't interfere with school study, you probably welcome a small introduction into the world of work to give them experience as well as the discipline involved in organizing their time. Make sure:

> ● that it doesn't involve **you** in extra work—no rousing him at 5 a.m.; provide an alarm clock instead: doing it himself is the name of the game
> ● that you know how the law stands about employment of young people
> ● Many jobs cannot be held by children under the age of 16, and working papers may be needed.

PAYING HIS OWN WAY

What about a contribution to the family budget once son or daughter becomes a full-time wage-earner? There are some parts of the country where it would still be in order for mom to take over the unopened wage packet or unemployment pay, and count out and return allowance, earmarking the rest for food, clothes or saving. But this is not good preparation for the time when he has to budget for himself.

Most parents suggest a weekly sum to be given to them for board. Should this be a token payment or represent a realistic contribution? One mother told me she charged her daughter what she would have had to pay for full board with a landlady, but most parents let heart rule head and err on the low side. If you can't bring yourself to charge very much, at least try to see that food costs are covered.

Go over prices with him to get it clear. Then stick to that charge. It's tempting to let him off for a week or two when he's needing a new jacket, or she wants a dress, but it won't help them in the long run, as no one else is going to let them off regular payments. Better charge a bit less and stick to it, or give a loan quite separate from these payments.

FOOTING THE WHOLE BILL

Even young people who pay a reasonable sum towards upkeep don't realize the full expense of going it alone. Our children were warned, before leaving home as students, of the hundred and one unexpected things they'd have to stump up for. Living at home, they can dip into family supplies when they:

- post a letter
- clean teeth
- clean shoes
- need an aspirin
- have a sore throat
- sew on a button

No one expects each member of the family to keep his own stock of shoe-cleaning materials or mouthwash. Yet all these items add up.

Where an education grant to students is to be supplemented by a parental contribution, those payments by parents are not an optional extra but are really needed. At the other extreme, giving them a lot over the odds is no kindness either. They are at university or college to work—not to spend money using their time in too many other ways.

PAYMENT FOR SERVICES RENDERED

Families aren't run on business lines, and it's a mistake for children to grow up thinking they are entitled to get money for every bit of help they give. Help is given in both directions out of love—or duty—and because belonging to a family means sharing and helping one another. But parents may want to pay for certain extra jobs done regularly or once in a while. It could be a thorough weekly clean of the car or an annual painting of the fence. Older teenagers may decorate a room or paint the house. One working mom I heard of has little time for housework, so pays her daughter to vacuum the house. You may prefer to cut out talk of money. 'You're saving my time cleaning the car, so can I give you a hand with anything later?' could be a better way of managing things.

CLOTHES

I remember apologizing to a shop assistant about a slight difference of opinion my daughter and I had had over a coat we were choosing for her. She waved aside my apology telling me it was nothing compared to the scenes she constantly witnessed between parents and teenagers. That was a few years ago, but I suspect that the question of choosing clothes is still a vexed one. Parents and teenagers are usually asking quite different questions.

PARENTS
- What will it cost?
- Will it last?
- Is it sensible?

TEENAGERS
- What is everyone else wearing?
- Will it make me feel good?
- Is it what I want right now?

Some compromise is needed. Talk over the dollars and cents before setting out for the shops. Work out, if you can, how much your overall budget can allow for clothes, then discuss with your teenager how it can be allocated. Young people are usually reasonable if given the facts. Here are some suggestions for trying to accommodate both sides:

- Buy cheap fashion garments or shoes (e.g. high-heeled shoes for short-time wear only, sensible shoes for the rest of the time)
- Buy cheap material and **make** fashion clothes (a mom I know helps her daughters do this)
- Expensive gear either as Christmas/birthday gifts or out of teenager's own savings or earnings

CARE OF CLOTHES

Most teenagers leave clothes lying just how and where they came off them! They can be shown that looking after clothes is half the secret of making them look good. There's no reason why they themselves shouldn't hang clothes up, wash special things separately, iron, mend or alter. Mom might do well to give simple instruction in washing of woollens, tights and undies, even though she continues to do the main wash.

FOOD

YOU ARE WHAT YOU EAT

How well you feel and how good you look depends a lot on what you eat. Food fanatics can be a pain in the neck but it *is* important to think about the family meals and plan carefully. There are a few basic rules worth following.

Quality not quantity counts Don't make unwilling eaters force down more than they can stomach, but see that the food offered contains *all* that they really need for health and energy. Some teenage appetites do call for plenty of 'fillers' of course, but still ensure that enough of the necessary foods are eaten.

Quality does not equal costly The most expensive foods—so-called 'convenience foods' (ready-frozen hamburgers, pies, chips or canned goods)—contain less goodness than a batch of home-made soup concocted from good bone stock, fresh vegetables and lentils or peas. Cheap cuts of meat have just as much food value as prime steaks. They just require a little more imagination and time to cook to perfection. And remember the importance of eye appeal: get enough color contrast and serve food attractively.

Cold foods—salads or packed meals—can be just as nutritious as hot meat and two veg. Cold food is just as warming to the body too: it's the food content that warms you, not the temperature.

Extravagance is out for all who are aware that many in the world are starving. Everyone has different ideas of what extravagance means, but it could include buying:

- foods highly priced because out of season
- luxury foods (e.g. expensive cream cakes, frozen cheesecakes)
- expensive meals out

Wasting food is also out. There are many ways of using up every kind of leftover to prepare delicious dishes.

WHICH FOODS?

For a balanced diet, you need to provide a selection of foods from each of the main food groups in the table overleaf for meals at home or for packed lunches.

Extra vitamins, except when prescribed by a doctor, are quite unnecessary when a balanced diet is followed.

The body also needs small quantities of minerals: calcium (for strong bones) is found in milk, cheese and nuts, and iron

Food group	Purpose served	Found in
proteins	body growth and tissue repair	fish, eggs, meat, milk, cheese, cereals, nuts, beans, lentils, peas
fats	keep you warm and active	butter, margarine, oils, meat, milk, cheese, fat, ice cream
carbohydrates	give energy and are good 'fillers'	sugar, potatoes, bread, cake, cereals, biscuits, root vegetables

The body also needs vitamins—tiny but vital ingredients to good health. These aren't manufactured by the body but are obtained from various foods.

Vitamin	Purpose served	Found in
A	healthy growth—prevents infection; healthy eyes—night vision	dairy products, eggs, fruit, vegetables
B	growth; health—helps body use other foods	wholewheat, oats, yeast, liver, eggs, meat, broth
C (ascorbic acid)	healing wounds, resisting infection; needed every day (body does not store it)	fruit—especially oranges, blackcurrants, salad, fresh vegetables
D	healthy teeth, strong bones	sunshine, oily fish, giblets, egg yolk, butter, margarine

(for healthy blood) can be obtained from liver, kidney, eggs, cocoa and green vegetables. Also required are fluids and roughage or fiber (in bran or wholemeal flour) which helps to prevent constipation and many other so-called 'Western diseases'.

Junk foods such as sweets, chips, cakes, cookies, 'pop' . . . would be happily eaten much of the time by some teenagers. Encourage cutting down on them because:

- they put on weight
- they cause tooth decay
- they encourage acne
- they fill up so that good food is not eaten at meals

WEIGHT-WATCHING

It's easy to get into the way of providing good filling meals, with plenty of bread, pastry, puddings, cakes, and to forget that it's not in anyone's interests, parents or teenagers, to put on too much weight. If you come from a 'stout' family, you are more likely to have a weight problem. Many girls and boys are anxious to stay slim and parents are often reaching the age when they put on pounds more quickly and shed them with difficulty. Try to cut out fattening foods, especially sugar.

There are so many slimming magazines and diet sheets available that it's not necessary to say more—except that any diet must include those vital foods already mentioned. Weight-watching may be good, but making a religion of the business of slimming is not. Jesus said, 'After all, isn't life worth more than food?' Eating too much, or thinking too much about your diet, can be giving food too big a place in life.

ANOREXIA NERVOSA

A number of parents may in fact be worrying on this very account. When does a normal concern about losing weight turn into the illness known as *anorexia nervosa*? People of all ages and both sexes can suffer from this, but it is far and away most common in girls—about one girl in every two hundred between the ages of sixteen and eighteen gets it. The causes are not yet fully understood, but complete cure *is* possible.

If you think your teenage daughter may be anorexic, there are some tell-tale symptoms to look out for. The sufferer is dissatisfied with herself and thinks she's too fat, however thin she may have become. She tries to slim excessively by going without food, exercising a lot and sometimes by taking purgatives. She may alternately starve and stuff (secretly). A feeling that she can't allow herself what she wants may affect spending patterns, leading to scrimping or else alternating bouts of penny-pinching and shop-lifting.

RESULTS AND RECOVERY

The emotional effects of the illness include feelings of dissatisfaction and isolation; the usual social pleasure of eating with others is denied. The results are excessive thinness, undernourishment, constipation and dizziness. In a girl, periods often stop. All these problems disappear once a good eating pattern is resumed.

It is *most* important that treatment is sought. See your doctor if you are concerned that this may be your daughter's problem. Hospital treatment may be advised. Much patience, love and a relationship that restores her self-confidence is needed at home.

HEALTH AND BEAUTY

Parents may worry about health and teenagers about beauty, but they really go hand in hand. A healthy person usually looks good too.

IMMUNIZATION

Most people know that if an expectant mother catches German measles, her unborn child may be seriously handicapped at birth. It is important that all girls be immunized against the disease, known as rubella, whether they think they have had the illness or not, before they start to menstruate. Generally this is given before a child enters school.

Diphtheria and tetanus Booster doses against these two diseases should be given between the ages of fourteen and sixteen.

HYGIENE

This is important both for health and attractiveness. You may need to drop gentle hints about the need for:

- **Clean hands:** always wash after going to the toilet and before touching food.
- **Clean nails:** dirt and germs can be trapped beneath dirty nails.
- **Clean hair:** wash at least once a week; if he or she wants it long, then they must be prepared for the extra trouble involved in washing, brushing and combing. Most young people keep their hair beautifully, but even clean hair can become infected by lice, especially when it's long.

● **Personal freshness:** wash between legs and under arms daily; use a deodorant. Wash feet, and change socks or tights daily.

● **Dental care:** frequent brushing with a good toothbrush, especially last thing at night, plus six-monthly visits to the dentist.

● **Skin care:** avoid junk foods; wash with a good medicated soap. If spots and acne are bad, see a doctor. It's important to make a real effort to clear up this troublesome area of teenage suffering if you can.

FURTHER INFORMATION

'The Pocket Guide to Babysitting', US Government Printing Office

'What About Nutrients in Fast Foods?' Free from the Consumer Information Center

The National Association of Anorexia Nervosa and Associated Disorders, Box 271, Highland Park, Ill. 60035

The Center for the Study of Anorexia and Bulimia, 1 West 91st St., New York, NY 10024

IN TROUBLE?

Sooner or later the truth is out—he or she is in trouble of some kind. So what do you do? Here are some of the ways in which parents react:

- 'Get out and don't come back!'
- 'Either you stop what you're doing or you leave this house.'
- 'We're sure it can't be **your** fault.'
- 'What have **we** done to deserve this behavior?'
- 'It's not him, it's his friends that get him into trouble.'
- 'If you want to mess up your life that's your affair.'
- 'It's got to stop, but we want to stand by you and help you all we can.'

Most of these reactions are natural. Parents either want to protect and defend, or to wash their hands altogether of the offending child. What matters is to shoulder the part of the responsibility that is yours—then help him to take the share that he must bear.

ALL YOURS
Whatever they may do, your children are *yours*. By birth (unless adopted) they have inherited your characteristics. By

law you are responsible for them. Even if they are legally of age, they haven't stopped being your children. To some extent, your upbringing has shaped them. Your pride may be hurt, your deepest feelings wounded, but you love them still and want to do what is best for *them*.

PARENTAL POLICY

Many parents make the mistake of blaming themselves too much for their child's mistakes. Others never think to criticize themselves or see that *they* may have been in the wrong too. Being too strict can make some young people react against parents and plunge into the very activities that have been so rigorously banned, but being too slack and letting a teenager have more freedom than he can handle can also be a disaster. So it's better to check up on yourselves at intervals before trouble comes. One parent may sometimes try to counteract over-firmness or over-indulgence on the part of the other. Much better to sort out a common policy, each giving a bit of ground, then play a joint, strong hand.

WHEN IT COMES TO THE CRUNCH

What really matters is being on the same side as your teenager, not in opposite camps. He may see you as the enemy when you disapprove, but he needs to know that you really care about what is best for him. Once problems arise, you are there to stand alongside him, not to bale him out painlessly but to give him the strength and support he needs to deal with the crisis.

TROUBLE WITH DRUGS

What would *you* call a drug? There are all kinds of possible answers.

It's a beverage Alcohol, of course; but tea, coffee, cocoa and *Coke* all contain the drug caffeine, and teenagers are sometimes quick to point out that mom is rushing to get her 'fix' when she puts on the kettle for that life-saving cuppa!

It's a medicine 'My doctor prescribed it'—and that may be true of a hundred and one things the doctor gives, including the mild tranquilizer or buck-me-up pill.

It's a nasty habit That's how a lot of people might describe smoking—but it's a drug too.

SMOKING

Children are beginning to smoke at a younger age, nowadays often by eight or nine. So it can be difficult to stop even as early as the teens. Why do they start? The reasons most often given are:

- because it's tough to smoke
- because it makes you feel grown-up
- because clever people usually do

We know that none of these reasons is remotely near the truth, but it's difficult to get rid of the image that smoking has had for years and which advertisements reinforce. Research has shown that in fact children are much more likely to become smokers (not just to try it out once) if:

- both parents smoke
- parents don't bother whether the child smokes or not
- older brother or sister smokes
- friends smoke
- he's not a 'high-flyer' at school

You may decide at this point that it's time you both stopped smoking for your child's sake. With such a strong motive you've a good chance of success.

DON'T DO IT!

Most teenagers know off by heart the link between smoking and lung cancer, but that doesn't seem to register as any real danger to *them*. Some of the reasons for not smoking include:

- **dangers:** lung cancer, heart disease, bronchitis, damage to unborn child when mother smokes
- **disadvantages:** costs a lot, makes you and your clothes smell stale (**not** very attractive to the opposite sex), spoils the taste of food

THE ANSWER IS PILL-SHAPED

'Got a headache? Take an aspirin.' It's easy to become a pill-popping family, and moms and dads who are always at the medicine-chest or the pharmacist's tend to have children who are the same. It has also been shown that parents who take drugs that are *legal* are much more likely to have children who take drugs that are *illegal*.

It's to be hoped that most doctors now recognize that tranquilizers are best prescribed for a very short emergency period only (for example, after a bereavement) and sleeping pills are best avoided altogether. Both types of drug can become addictive and sleeping tablets carry the risk of a small margin between a safe dose and a fatal overdose, especially when combined with alcohol.

The Bible has a sensible prescription for worry (not, of course, the chronic depression which needs specialist medical treatment): 'Tell God every detail of your needs in earnest and thankful prayer,' advises the apostle Paul, 'and the peace of God . . . will keep constant guard over your hearts and minds as they rest in Christ Jesus.'

JUST TO MAKE THE PARTY GO?

Get the facts about alcohol clear for yourselves and see that your children know them too. The increase in drunkenness and alcoholism (two different things) is alarming. Fatal accidents and crime are two of the by-products. Many Christians feel it is not right for them to drink. Others feel they are free to drink in moderation. Parents of teenagers can help by:

- setting the right example in their own use of alcohol
- making their views (and reasons for them) known to their children
- making reasonable rules about drinking, especially where driving/drinking is involved
- waiting until they are in their teens before letting children drink alcohol, then letting them try it at home, perhaps diluted at first or with a meal
- making it plain that fun, friendliness and happiness are all possible **without** the help of alcohol

Alcoholism is a disease affecting some people. There is no way of knowing in advance who could become one, but it now seems that 'an alcoholic is more likely to have a mother, father or more distant relative who is an alcoholic'. If the body has this predetermined tendency to the disease, extra precautions and explanations will be necessary in your family.

FACTS ABOUT TEENAGE DRINKING
Teenagers are more likely to drink when:

- parents give too much allowance
- both parents work in the evenings, leaving them at a loose end
- both parents campaign too vigorously for total abstinence

It's an interesting fact that youngsters who go to church-related organizations drink less than those attending discos, dances or (naturally) bars. This is one more reason why your child might want to hook into a Youth for Christ or Young Life group which provides on-the-go activities that can engage the energies and attention of teens in a wholesome environment.

THE DRUG SCENE
What most parents have in mind when they worry about their teenagers getting hooked on drugs are substances that are:

- able to affect moods and thinking processes
- taken specially in order to get 'high'
- against the law

Most people are aware of the danger of so-called 'hard drugs'. Heroin is particularly dangerous in that the difference between a safe dose and a fatal one is small, and it is impossible to judge the size of the dose since black market heroin is never pure.

THE BIG QUESTION MARK
Many young people who would not dream of taking hard drugs argue with parents that there is nothing wrong with smoking 'pot' or marijuana. However, there is still a big question mark over this drug. No one is certain yet what the long-term effects may be (though it probably *is* safer than tobacco and alcohol). Those taking pot *are* more likely to go on to heroin, perhaps because they tend to move in the same circles as hard drug

users. And smoking pot *is* against the law, whatever young people may think of that law. This last fact clinches the matter. No parent will want to see their child break the law and suffer the results.

SOLVENT ABUSE

This is often referred to as 'glue-sniffing', but other things besides glue may be used, including cleaning fluids. Most glue-sniffers are in the ten to fifteen age-group. The problem is that the practice is not illegal and no one can prevent children from buying glue. Signs of solvent abuse are a change in personality, smell and stains of glue on clothes and spots around the nose and mouth.

HOW WILL YOU KNOW?

How can we recognize the symptoms of other kinds of drug-taking? It's impossible to give a comprehensive list. They can be so varied that both loss of appetite or increased appetite could be tell-tale signs. Not all drugs cause pin-point pupils, though a glazed look in the eyes is common. Once again, the best test for a parent is a change in personality. Perhaps a youngster who has normally been polite and quiet becomes aggressive, or a cheerful, outgoing one becomes silent and withdrawn. A teacher may spot the signs and talk to you, or you may wish to confide your fears to an understanding head teacher.

A child who is taking drugs will need your help as well as your firm handling of the situation. You can't condone drug-taking any more than you would any law-breaking, or belittle the damage he is doing himself.

IN TROUBLE: SEX

'I'm going to have a baby.' Whatever your shock, or anger, now is not the time or place for lectures, abuse or recrimination. It's too late for that. She is probably feeling sick, afraid and desperately in need of support and loving care. So what are you going to say?

- 'He'll have to marry you.'
- 'You'll have to have an abortion'.
- 'The baby will have to be adopted'.
- 'You'll have to go away from here.'
- 'Don't worry—we'll look after the baby for you.'

Now is not the time to make any of those far-reaching decisions. Stop and think—and pray together first. Then you may want to get advice from someone with experience in such matters and enough care to give support and information. The organization 'Birthright' does just this. They offer a free pregnancy test, free doctor visit, and emotional and material support that will encourage a girl to carry the baby and not resort to abortion. They are in your local phone book or write for the branch nearest you: Birthright, 686 N. Broad St, Woodbury, NJ 08096.

LOOK BEFORE YOU LEAP

There are many factors to be taken into account.

Abortion (taking the life of an unborn child) is not a justifiable action simply to rid you of your problem or embarrassment. While marriage—however unsuited or incompatible the partners—may have been the answer the previous generation would have given, an unhappy marriage won't put matters right for the unborn child or for his parents.

If you take over total responsibility, so that you are both left literally 'holding the baby', you will not be helping your daughter to mature or to learn from experience. But don't opt out; in this situation, parents as well as teenage daughter are going to have to suffer the consequences of *her* action.

SEXUALLY-TRANSMITTED DISEASES

Not all of these are the result of 'sleeping around'. But all are passed on *only* through sexual contact (*not* by using public lavatories). If two people who are free of such a disease get married, neither can catch it. So the only way to be sure of avoiding VD is to avoid casual sex. If your teenager gets any symptoms that could mean he is infected, he must get treatment at once. Insist on a check-up, if only for reassurance. In most towns there are special clinics where patients can be seen without an appointment or letter from a doctor.

TROUBLE WITH THE LAW

If police arrive at *your* front door to charge your teenager with shop-lifting, football hooliganism or house-breaking, shock will be your first reaction.

NOW WHAT?

You have a dual role. Naturally, as parents, you will fly to your child's defence. It may indeed be that he has got in with the wrong crowd. But you must also support law and order. You cannot shield him from the results of his actions. You may want to get a lawyer to see that he is represented in the best possible light. Or you may want to consult a lawyer, for a small fee, to find out your best course of action. Your local Citizens' Advice Bureau will have a list. At some CAB branches, a lawyer gives so much time per week for freely advising clients.

If you are not represented in court by a lawyer, the clerk of the court will represent your teenager's case to the magistrates. Others who might offer helpful advice or support are your minister or a social worker. There may be someone in your local church fellowship with expertise and the ability to listen and counsel.

FURTHER INFORMATION

Families Anonymous, PO Box 344, Torrance, Calif. 90501 (a support group similar to Al Anon, but for families of drug abusers)

The National Institute of Drug Abuse Clearing House, NIDA, Rockville, Md. 20850 (provides a list of 3,500 drug treatment programs)

'National Directory of Children and Youth Services', CPR Directory Services Co., Washington, DC (ask for this hefty reference book at your library)

Government publications on drug abuse available from: NCDAI, PO Box 416, Kensington, Md. 20795

Government publications on alcohol abuse available from: NCALI, 1776 East Jefferson St., Plaza S., 4th floor, Rockville, Md. 20852

Mothers Against Drunk Driving, 5330 Primrose, Suite 146, Fair Oaks, Calif. 95628

National Runaway Hotline: 1-800-361-4000. Toll-free number will give you or your child information about help available in your local area.

National VD Information Number (toll-free): 1-800-227-8922

WHAT NEXT?

Perhaps you've got it all lined up: 'He'll be a plumber like I am', or 'She'll be a teacher like her mom'. You may take it for granted that he'll leave school as soon as he's old enough or else assume that she'll go on to university. But you're just as likely to have no idea what your teenager will be doing in a year or two because *he* hasn't a clue.

PREPARING FOR COLLEGE

You may have at least two years of advanced education in mind for your child.

Many larger counties support a community college which gives an associate's degree (AAS). These schools are affordable to most families and offer extensive transferable credits. They may or may not have dormitory facilities, as most of their students are within easy commuting distance. Community colleges provide an excellent opportunity for students to see if they are college material. Today many technical careers are open to people with an AAS.

Four-year private and public colleges offer a bachelor's degree in arts and sciences (BA or BS). Private schools tend to cost more than the state-supported schools.

WHERE TO START

An eleventh grader may apply for early college acceptance, but most students apply in the fall of their senior year. Choosing the right school for your child may follow:

- a college night where many college representatives are available to give necessary information and catalogs
- reading college information sent after taking the SATs or ACTs
- visiting a college with his high school class
- putting his interests into the Guidance Information System computer and reading the print-outs that match his interests and abilities

The following books may be of help:

- 'Lovejoy's Career and Vocational School Guide', Simon and Schuster
- 'Lovejoy's College Guide'
- 'The College Handbook', College Entrance Examination Book
- 'Index of Majors', College Entrance Examination Book
- 'Barron's Profile of American Colleges', Barron's Educational Series, Inc.
- 'Barron's Profile of American Colleges', Vol. II—Index of College Majors
- 'Chronicle Student Aid Annual', Chronicle Guidance
- 'Chronicle Two-Year College Data Book'
- 'Chronicle Four-Year College Data Book'
- 'Chronicle Vocational School Manual'

PREPARING FOR WORK

Who *does* decide your son's or daughter's future? Is it a matter of:

- what the school advises?
- what **you** decide?
- what **he** wants to do?

Some young people have quite definite ideas about what they want to do or be. Whatever his feelings, try to sort out ideas together by talking about all the possibilities—discussing, getting information and praying. Be honest and realistic, both about opportunities *and* his ability. If he is not a good student, it's not very sensible to consider a university course, unless the school has strong reasons for thinking otherwise. If he has scored a good number of high grade courses, think twice before insisting he leaves school immediately.

Make use of every opportunity given to discuss his future with the guidance staff. They know his abilities and the kind of study and job prospects, and can take a more detached view. If higher education seems advisable, find out the costs.

MAKING UP HIS MIND

Discover what scope there is in the kind of work that interests him. Work out your priorities—and his—in planning for his future. Which comes top of the list? Security? Money? Happiness? Fulfilment? Usefulness to others? Remember:

- Training and the right job are as important for girls as boys.
- Leisure time will make up an increasingly large part of life: he needs to be equipped to enjoy and use this for himself and others too.
- Security may not be top priority with young people and is very hard to forecast anyway. Most young people may need to retrain at least once in their life.
- A job that gives satisfaction and fulfilment may not be well-paid.

CAREERS ADVICE

Most schools provide careers advice, and some arrange visits of a day or longer to various places of work, so that young people can see for themselves and even try out a job. Advice is usually given by:

Careers teacher who is specially appointed and allowed lesson-time to advise and help. He will have leaflets and guides to give information.

Teachers—their reports give you a good idea of your teenager's particular strong subjects.

Guidance counselor who will have an overall

picture of him, gained from teachers' reports and his own experienced observations.

Career resource center—will no doubt include *Encyclopedia of Careers* (Doubleday), *Occupational Outlook Handbook* (US Dept. of Labor), *Dictionary of Occupational Titles* (US Dept. of Labor), and *Guidance Information System* (Houghton Mifflin).

CHOOSING A JOB

It's no good being too limited in ideas when looking for a job at present. Many young people are just glad to get work—any work at all. But, if at all possible, a girl or boy will want to get work that interests them and gives scope for using their own abilities. Why not let him compile a list of interests and conditions preferred?

> ● **What are you good at?** Using my hands—typing, cookery, woodwork/English or calculations/languages or science subjects
> ● **Who are you good with?** People my own age/old people/children
> ● **Where do you want to work?** Outdoors/hospital/school/factory/department store
> ● **Home or away?** Prepared to commute each day/ready to live away from home
> ● **What hours?** Strictly 9–5/shift work/nights

It's well worth thinking these things out before getting careers advice as it gives the adviser concrete facts to work from. Then try to discover what scope there is within the limits set. For example, in medical work there could be openings as: doctor, nurse, orderly, physiotherapist, chiropodist, porter, clerical worker.

LEAVE OR STAY ON?

Many parents who take it for granted that a child will leave school and start bringing something into the kitty after graduation may find it hard to accept that a son or daughter should want to spend another three to five years without earning and at considerable expense to them. At the other extreme, there are parents who set their heart on higher education and one of the professions and find it hard to swallow the fact that their teenager would be happier leaving school. But

STAYING-ON: FULL-TIME EDUCATION

For	Against
Better qualified, wider job choice and better chance of a job	Dependent on parents for longer time
Enjoyment of the course	If no further qualification gained, can be harder to get job a year later
More mature, when older, to decide job	Further study not enjoyed by all

LEAVING SCHOOL AT SIXTEEN

For	Against
Getting paid	Very young to decide future
Less dependent on parents	Missing opportunities that higher education brings in jobs
Part-time training can be taken while you work	Combining study and training with work can be tough

what matters most? Your pride? Your pocket? Or his best interests and happiness?

Some of the arguments put forward in the leave-or-stay-on debate are set out above.

JOB-HUNTING

Watching want ads, letting friends and relatives know of availability, registering at public and private employment offices and civil service offices are all good tips when a youth is ready for steady employment.

LETTER OF APPLICATION

Remember that *his* letter may be one of hundreds. Unless he gives a good impression, he will never get as far as an interview. So make sure that the form provided or the paper used goes off clean and carefully written (no blots or spelling mistakes).

Make sure he:

- puts facts simply and clearly
- is courteous but not cringing
- begins and ends a letter correctly ('Dear Sir' should end 'Yours faithfully' and 'Dear Mr Smith' ends 'Yours sincerely')

INTERVIEW

Help him to go off calmly and in good time. Suggest that he dresses to suit the occasion—it's not a night at the disco. Cleanness, neatness, well-brushed shoes and well-pressed clothes all reflect a person who will do a good job. Don't take away his confidence—tell him he looks good. Make sure he:

- knows a bit about the firm concerned
- is polite but not too polite!
- is himself—natural and honest as far as nervousness allows
- is ready to ask questions about the job or course

OUT OF WORK

God gave man work to do from the word go, and to be deprived of a job is to be deprived of a real human right. But more and more young people, as well as older ones, are being left high and dry in the job market. Some of the effects of unemployment are:

- depression, leading in some cases to suicide
- isolation: feeling cut off from others who have jobs
- lack of identity: anyone's first question is 'What's your job?' or 'Where do you work?'
- sense of failure: no one wants them

If your son or daughter is unemployed, they need extra encouragement at home to reassure them that they *do* matter. They also badly need work of some kind.

JOB TRAINING PARTNERSHIP ACT

Replacing CETA, the new legislation JTPA will put young people to work in the private sector for 250 hours of subsidized employment, and then it is hoped the employer will put the youth on its payroll. A youth, to be enrolled in this program, must meet federal guide-lines.

The advantages of going on this program are:

- **the chance to gain experience:** there is a certificate at the end and it can be a big help to claim experience when applying for a job
- **some money in his pocket:** a minimum allowance is given
- **the opportunity to try out a job** and perhaps discover where his interests lie

PREPARING TO LEAVE HOME

Sooner or later your son or daughter will leave home. It may be as a student, or because his firm transfers him to another part of the country. He or she may want to set up in their own flat or plan to get married. *Your* job is to see that they are properly equipped to fend for themselves, and that calls for planning in advance. How good are they at the everyday jobs involved in running a home and in organizing their own lives? Can they:

- cook a nourishing and not too expensive meal?
- mend and make clothes? (Sons should be able to sew and repair as well as daughters)
- clean a room, wash, dry and iron clothes so that they aren't ruined?
- do simple decorating, mend a fuse?
- shop economically?
- balance a checkbook?

Can they take care of themselves? Can they:

- cope with colds/cuts/general first aid?
- look after general appearance without constant reminders?
- keep kitchen/bathroom clean and hygienic?

How used are they to:

- making their own appointments (dentist, hairdresser) and cancelling when necessary?
- apologizing and thanking?
- taking their own decisions about what to eat or wear, when to go to bed?

This may sound very elementary, but one teenager told me how tiring and strange it was making her own routine when she first went to university. She came from a home where there was a fairly rigid pattern of meals and bedtimes and she found it strange to be responsible for herself. Some young people let it go to their heads and stay up to all hours, go without proper meals and generally throw off restraint. So some freedom to create their own pattern while at home could help.

Do you still wake him each morning or remind him to return his library book before that fine is due? Sooner or later he has to be responsible for himself, so a gradual change to 'do it yourself' is called for.

THINKING OF OTHERS

Some parents put up with a good deal of selfishness and lack of consideration from a teenage son or daughter. Others won't be so tolerant. It's no kindness to bring a child up expecting everyone to care only about *his* happiness. He's in for a rude awakening. If he lives in a hostel or shares a flat with others, he'll be expected to take his share of unpleasant chores and make an effort not to disturb others by noisy late nights or by behaving in any way that cuts across their interests.

PAVING THE WAY

Of course you will want to make things as smooth as you can when he first leaves home. Most parents would be anxious about letting their eighteen-year-old take a job in another part of the country. You may want to go and look over the apartment for yourself as well as taking the newcomer and his belongings safely to the new destination. There is all the difference in the world between over-protecting your children and leaving them open to danger or exploitation. You have to strike the right balance.

Addresses of friends You may have an old friend or some distant relation who lives not too far away from the new center. Provide the address and phone number in case of emergency or loneliness, but without extracting too many promises to make contact.

Church contact You may belong to a church that makes it a practice to link members to a church in their new area. If not, ask for details of a kindred church in the new neighborhood. Again, you should feel free to provide information, but don't insist that he attend the same denomination as you. The choice is now his.

Students Inter-Varsity Christian Fellowship (233 Langdon St., Madison,Wisc. 53703), Campus Crusade for Christ (National Campus Office, Arrowhead Springs, Calif. 92414), Navigators (PO Box 6000, Colorado Springs, Colo. 80934) and/or many denominational ministries have programs at nearly every college campus. You might want to ask the ministry to contact your child, so as to make the acquaintance easy.

Getting a glimpse The book *Leaving Home: The Making of an Independent Woman* by Evelyn Bence (Westminster Press/Bridgebooks, Philadelphia, Pa.) takes a good look at the ambivalent feelings many young women have to sort out during and after high school and after college years. They want a life of their own, yet the big wide world seems, at times, terrifying. Many feel 'homeless' until they marry. Parents might find this book helpful in making sense of the late-night phone calls that tempt you to say 'I'm coming to get you and bring you back here where I can take care of you'. Remember, you are your single child's closest relative. They may be doing just fine, yet need you to let them blow off steam.

PREPARING FOR MARRIAGE

This preparation won't take the form of a cosy little half-hour chat. We've mentioned several times the effect your own marriage will have as a visual aid. Your views on marriage, as they crop up in conversation, will have an effect too. You will want to make plain that:

- **Marriage is for keeps:** the Christian view of marriage is not 'stick it till you get fed up'
- **Both partners need to be of the same mind** on important matters; above all, a Christian needs a Christian partner
- **Barriers** of age, social class or mental ability may put extra stress on a marriage but **are not impossible to overcome**; race or color difference is no hindrance to a happy marriage, provided that the added difficulties have been fully faced and there is real love and oneness of heart and mind.
- **Being good friends** as well as good lovers matters in marriage.

MARRIAGE AS THE GOAL?

Perhaps too many parents (moms especially?) like to get their daughters married off. They put pressure on them to start courting and talk as if marriage is the only goal to be aimed at. Some mothers see it as a reflection on themselves if their daughter hasn't a boy-friend. Fathers, too, might remark to a son that 'When I was your age I was taking a nice girl out, not studying books'. Be thankful if your teenager is happy with friends of both sexes and prefers to leave going steady for a few years yet. He'll be older and wiser then.

GAINING A SON, GAINING A DAUGHTER

Some young people bring home a succession of boy- and girl-friends, while others say nothing until they arrive with the person they plan to marry. Try to adopt the right kind of welcome—warm, without jumping to definite conclusions. Don't look on every arrival as a future son- or daughter-in-law. Do try to give the welcome that any friend of either sex might expect from loving and interested parents.

It's worth remembering that since they were tiny, one critical word from you about a friend increased their keenness and loyalty to him. So it's not even good *policy* to make disparaging remarks about the boy- or girl-friend! Good parents may feel that they should point out their reasons for thinking that a particular friendship could not result in a happy marriage. But that said, they are free to choose, and it would be tragic to lose a son or daughter by hasty or strong-worded criticism of a future husband or wife. Surely it's better to keep your son and daughter plus a not-perfect partner than to lose both for ever? And, anyway, would you think anyone quite good enough for your child? So look for the best in their attachments and work at your new relationships.

FURTHER INFORMATION

'Student Guide—Five Federal Financial Aid Programs', free booklet from
    Consumer Information Center, Dept. L, Pueblo, Colo. 81009
Financial Aid Planning, Box 1904, Radio City Station, New York,
    NY 10101 (for information about meeting college expenses)
'Christian Career Planning', John D. Bradley (Multnomah Press)
'Campus Life' magazine and 'Christian Herald' magazine each runs
    its own 'Guide to Christian colleges' in October issues.

INDEPENDENCE

To you they'll always be 'the children', and in one sense your child is your child for ever. But it's time to recognize that your home now contains three, four, five or more adults. It's no longer 'them and us' in quite the same way—they have grown up. Dad no longer takes it for granted that his views are right and theirs not worth a hearing. Mom doesn't say any more 'Run and fetch . . .' or 'Mind your muddy feet'. At least, we hope not. Instead you aim at discussion, responsibility and acceptance of everyone's right to their own life. This can mean the 'children' doing a bit of readjusting too!

INDEPENDENCE—MOVING AWAY

Janet has left home to go to college. She plans to share an apartment with three other students. How much will her parents keep track of her?

● **Check constantly:** phone several times a week, go down at week-ends; find out how she spends leisure, what her friends are like. Ask each other each day 'I wonder how Janet is managing? What will she be doing today?'

● **Leave her to it:** 'It was her choice. We've done our bit and we're still paying out; it's up to her to work hard and make a go of it.'

● **Give background support:** 'We're here if you need us. We expect you will cope but let us know if you can't. We'll write regularly and you can phone and reverse the charge if you want a word. We'll come and see you and meet your friends if you think it a good idea, but shan't expect an invitation'.

If children want to kick over the traces they will do so, and there's no way you can stop them once they've left home. So it's better to let go, trust them—and God—and provide a home that's a good solid rock, the sort of foundation they need, and a safe, secure place to return to.

A DIFFERENT PERSON?

At home things have gone on unchanged—though more calmly —until the great day when the wanderer is first expected back. Great preparations are made to welcome son or daughter, perhaps for Christmas. Then in walks a new person, talking and behaving in a strange and surprising way. It's never quite the same person who went away. They eat different foods, scorn television programs once watched and have fresh views on every topic raised. If you have been prepared for the shock, you may both be able to sit tight and keep quiet until the worst is over. After a few days things will settle down, and signs of the familiar son or daughter will begin to re-emerge. You may be able to make a few tactful comments by then, but try to avoid an almighty bust-up on that first night home.

A PLACE OF HIS OWN

'I'd like an apartment of my own but mom would think it was awful. She'd either jump to the conclusion I wanted to do something she doesn't approve of, or she'd feel hurt to think I didn't want to go on living at home.'

If your son or daughter wants to have a place of their own *in the same district*, what's your reaction? Are you hurt? Incredulous? Suspicious? Disapproving?

It's easy to suspect the worst, or to wonder how on earth

he could prefer the expense of a cold damp 'pad' with no washing-machine or central heating to the comfort of your home. Does he dislike you that much?

The fact is that the need to be free to make your own decisions and create your own home is very strong in human beings. Some young people have the sense not to rush into marriage just for the sake of achieving that freedom yet want to strike out on their own. Isn't it reasonable? And, on second thoughts, wouldn't it be rather pleasant to have him as a near neighbor instead of a too-near lodger?

I speak from experience: one son of ours lives in his own small house about five miles away. He hasn't all the mod cons we enjoy and he has his own meals to get and cleaning to do, but he's free to plan his own life. We phone often, visit one another and thoroughly enjoy a relationship unspoiled by the minor irritations and cross purposes that living in one small bungalow, day in and day out, can cause.

'I'M TOO LAZY'

Stephen told me that he'd left home and had his own flat when he worked as a hairdresser fifty miles away. Now he's back in the district and has moved in again with his parents. He admits it isn't easy. He has a good many rows with his mother rather than buckle down to being at her beck and call. 'I ought to get a place of my own again,' he admits, 'but it's too comfortable having my meals cooked and getting lifts in their car. I just can't be bothered.' Parents may even need to give the fledgelings a bit of a push out of the nest rather than trying to keep them too warm and cosy.

INDEPENDENCE AT HOME

Ever get the feeling that there are too many bulls in your herd? Young males tend to pit their strength or aggression against dad, who in turn may resent the newly-grown contenders. Mom too may feel threatened by the appearance of daughters who make her seem decidedly older and less attractive.

Readjustment is needed all round. Parents' change of attitude must be matched by the young people's courtesy and consideration towards them. In practice, children who have never lived away from home find it very difficult to realize or appreciate just how much is being done to provide a comfortable home. Sometimes it's a matter of waiting until they discover by fending for themselves.

PEACEFUL CO-EXISTENCE?

What should parents' reactions be to the kind of situations that can crop up if everyone is to be free to live their own life?

- **Friends:** Are they to bring home friends you don't like or approve of?
- **Routine:** Should you have to arrange special mealtimes to suit them?
- **Late nights:** Do you wait downstairs or lie awake worrying?
- **Church:** Do you insist on Christian observance and church-going?
- **Standards:** Do you allow parties (with unlimited drink) to be held in your absence?

Look at the following reactions to such matters and check the one nearest to your view:

- **It's our home**—if they want to live here, they toe the line and fit in with us.
- **It's their home too**—they're free to have their own friends and way of life.
- **We share this home**—we'll give them freedom as far as we can. But where our own standards are concerned, they must respect our decision.
- **We'll get round the table and talk out each tricky situation.** In some cases **we** shall have a casting vote; but we'll give them the chance to put their viewpoint and fit in wherever possible. We'll share responsibility as well as decision making.

BALING THEM OUT—HOME OR AWAY

How far should parents go in providing a kind of fail-safe system for adult children? Fathers may be ready to let a son or daughter shoulder responsibility; mothers may undo his policy behind the scenes. Parents do need to act together. But if you have been used to writing notes to excuse him homework, keeping her off school with a headache, or giving extra

allowance whenever they ran short, you are going to find it
hard now to resist hints to:

- decorate his apartment
- look after her dog
- clean/wash/iron for him
- help with the next instalment on the bike or car
- lend him **your** car

Remember: a bit of help may be appreciated but a lot of regular
shouldering of their duties will be unappreciated, *and* will hinder
their development into mature people.

INDEPENDENCE FOR PARENTS

After years of planning, budgeting and thinking with the
children in mind, you are going to be independent again. Well
—perhaps not quite independent, but at least the time is
drawing near when you will be free most of the time from the
restrictions that the family has brought in the past.

PERPETUAL MOMS

One mother I know of has never stopped being a mom. She
has eight children. Her younger boys are still at home needing
to be looked after, the older ones have married and now have
families of their own. Because nearly all live near her, she is on
constant call. If she tries to get a morning out, there are
indignant cries of, 'Where were you? I phoned and called and
you were out.'

Some children, however grown-up, expect mom to man
the phone and home for twenty-four hours a day. Of course,
it's up to mom to decide whether or not she wants that sort of
role. She may love helping with the next generation of babies,
having everyone to Sunday dinner and generally being the
linchpin of the enlarged family circle. There is real satisfaction in
such a way of life. But not everyone wants that pattern.

Some husbands may have been looking forward to the day
when they could have the time and company of a wife who has
spent many years in childcare. Other women want a life and

interests of their own. Parents have (almost!) as much right to be independent as their children. Perhaps every parent is secretly glad when an occasional cry for help comes from one of the family, as long as it *is* occasional.

TIME ON YOUR HANDS?

What's to be done with this new-found freedom? Don't be surprised if at first you don't welcome it as you feel you should. It's hard to let go of your children and recognize that all those shared years of childcare and parenting are over.

I'd not realized how I was cherishing the past until I was jolted into the present by a move from the old family house to a compact bungalow devoid of all memories. There were no rooms that had once belonged to the children, no shared past— that window they were always breaking, the garden path where knees were cut open. I suddenly had to come to terms with the fact that a whole slice of my life was over.

At first there seemed no future to make. And this can be the reaction, even when a mother has a job of her own. Perhaps it hits her more than her husband as she has most often been the one to feed, nurse, comfort and work for the making of the home. It's important to find a new role. It takes courage and sometimes time, but it's 100 per cent worth the effort—for the sake of the mother herself, the happiness of the marriage and of the children too.

MARRIAGE RENOVATION

At last there is a chance to do things together. You may want to:

- do together the things you used to do: talk, listen to music, go for walks
- do some new things: take up bird-watching or archaeology, meet new people together as husband and wife
- use your home in a new way: for young people from church, the elderly, your own friends

Physical togetherness is important too. A team of American marriage advisers has come up with the discovery that 'touching is important as a means of keeping couples loving and close'!

Sadly, what came naturally at the beginning of your relationship has gradually gone by default. The presence in a small home of observant teenagers may have inhibited your freedom in making love. Now you are free to develop again your physical closeness without embarrassment or interruption.

SPIRITUAL SHARING

This is a time of strangely mixed feelings. There can be regret about aims not achieved and now never likely to be. This may be particularly true for a husband in his career or job. You still have longings to make something better of your life together. Share these feelings together and share them with God too. Why not devote an evening to talking and praying about your fears, your hopes, your concerns for the family and your plans for the future, rather than watching television? You will feel strengthened both as individuals and a team.

IT'S DIFFERENT FOR ME

Perhaps you fall outside the cosy twosome described above. A lone parent may face the prospect of a child leaving home with the knowledge that it will mean living alone for the first time. You will need even more courage to come to terms with this new stage, but you will probably be only too aware of the temptation to hold on to your child and will be determined to give him emotional freedom as well as letting him leave home.

You may need to consider taking someone into your home, for financial help or to relieve the sense of being alone. You probably have a job already but you may still need some new outlet which will provide added stimulus and new interests.

THE OLD FOLK

More and more couples are getting their children off their hands only to be faced with the burden of ageing parents. Caring for elderly relatives is described by the apostle Paul as being part of a Christian's loving duty. But it can be hard for a couple emerging from the demanding tasks of bringing up their family to be faced with dependent parents. The 'for and against' of old people's homes has to be worked out individually but it is important that your own marriage should not be harmed or worn down by the demands and intrusion of the older generation.

MOMS AT WORK!

I've never heard a woman admit to having too little to do. Yet boiled down, that hectic week may consist of a round of unnecessary housework. Carpets don't need daily vacuuming, nor paintwork a weekly wash, when there are no longer any

grubby hands or feet to bring in constant dirt. Other moms still go daily to the shops or drink coffee endlessly. Christians see time as a gift from God to be used wisely in worthwhile activity. Some husbands may now be at the busiest point of their working life. Others may be forced onto 'short time' or faced with early retirement. So a bit of extra money may be needed, or scope of some kind to do a worthwhile job.

Many women who have not worked outside the home lack confidence. They need to remember that they are not 'only a housewife'. Theirs are considerable skills as a nurse, dressmaker, home improver, cook, organizer, flower arranger and cleaner.

On top of such acquired skills, a housewife may have some rather rusty qualification left over from the days before the family. If her trade or profession is short-staffed, it may be easy to get a job quickly. If not, here are some suggestions:

Paid work Look out for ads in local papers.

Further training Contact your local adult education center for helpful, practical courses that can rekindle interest in hobbies or be used to bring in extra money. Contact the continuing education department of a nearby college or university for courses that will help you enter or return to a professional career. Many offer extension courses off campus. You also might want to contact them about enrolling full-time in a degree program.

Your possibilities are endless. You can contact a secretarial school, a nurses' training program, even a seminary, or you can contact home or party selling representatives and find out if your locale needs covering. You don't know how to sell? Their area representatives will help you out.

ALL FOR LOVE

It's a great pity that so many jokes and sour comments are made about so-called 'do-gooders' who give voluntary help in so many ways. There's an image of the middle-aged upper-middle-class Lady Bountiful who dispenses coffee and doughnuts to reluctant paupers, or sells white elephants at a church fair. Nothing could be further from reality.

All kinds of women, from every social group and with

every kind of skill—or no skills in particular—are needed desperately in every part of the country. You'll probably be surprised to discover the scope if you begin to inquire about outlets in your area. If you can scrub a floor, drive a car, arrange flowers, make tea, play with children, do clerical work, garden, decorate, weigh babies or sell magazines, you are sure of a job that's worthwhile. Here's how to find out what's going in your area:

> • **United Way:** Call your local chapter to ask what member organizations need help.
> • **Church:** Most churches have specific good-will projects which need help. They could put you in contact with inner-city ministries and para-church organizations.

HOSPITALS

The large hospital near us has a special member of staff to co-ordinate voluntary work in the hospital—work such as serving in the hospital shop, helping in the geriatric ward, looking after children in out-patients while mom sees the specialist, playing with child patients. Many special skills can be used. If you were a hairdresser, you could give a much-needed boost to patients' morale in so-called short-stay wards by doing their hair. The psychiatric ward needs volunteers with skills too.

Although there surely are no guarantees, hospital volunteers may be considered for jobs that open up. As you hone your skills, people are noticing your capabilities. What starts out as a volunteer project, may turn into a vocation.

'A CUP OF COLD WATER'

Jesus promised a reward to those who gave a cup of cold water in his name to a needy person. In such a dry and hot land, cold water could mean a lot. It involved a journey to the well for the one who gave it, or a share in their own precious stock.

Christians can sometimes help best by working as a group. Hospitals prefer a group to offer to visit elderly patients with no visitors of their own. It means that if one person can't go, another in the group can cover for them. A group from your church might organize such visiting.

You may find that all your free time can be used in the

fellowship of the local church. There may be elderly, housebound and disabled people to care for and others to have to your home.

A NEW FAMILY?

Perhaps you are both very fond of children and feel you were at your best raising your family. Why not continue the good work? There is a crying need for parents—or a single parent—to adopt or foster older children, and your age need not be a barrier.

Adopting means making a child as much your own as if he had been born to you; fostering involves working as part of a team headed by a social worker and including the child's parents. You are paid an allowance for looking after a child, and the arrangement may be on a short- or long-term basis.

There is probably more scope for fostering than adoption at your stage. Experienced parents who have brought up a family of their own are desperately needed to use their skills and love to provide home life for an older child. Make an appointment to see a social worker at your local Social Services office; a full list of adoption societies will be available there too.

FURTHER INFORMATION

'Checklist for Going into Business', free booklet from Consumer Information Center, Dept. L., Pueblo, Colo. 81009

'Job-Finding Techniques for Mature Women', US Government Printing Office, Washington, DC 20402

The National Center for Citizen Involvement, PO Box 4179, Boulder, Colo. 80306

The National Committee for Adoption, 1346 Connecticut Ave NW, Suite 326, Washington, DC 20036

JOB COMPLETED?

There's great satisfaction in standing back and surveying a job well done and at last completed. Looking at the newly-installed radiators or the birthday cake iced and decorated brings a feeling of achievement that makes all the hard work worthwhile. Can parents expect to feel the same about their children? Does there come a time when you can breathe a sigh of relief, step back, and agree that you've completed your task of bringing up the family successfully?

A lot may depend on what you were aiming for. Here are some goals you may have achieved. You may have brought up a son or daughter who is:

- an adult able to cope with life
- someone who can be at ease with others wherever they go
- happily married and settled in their own home
- more of a success in life than you have been
- happy and content

WAIT FOR IT!

But perhaps you aren't the satisfied customer. Becoming an adult is the beginning, not the end of the story. Your upbringing has given them the starting-point at which they can take over and continue for themselves. Parents aim to send their sons and daughters out into the world mature enough to be able to continue the process themselves in all the experiences that follow. Parents have tried to help their child to develop:

- **in body:** to be healthy, well-nourished, have practical skills
- **in mind:** having reached their own peak—neither forced to study beyond their ability, nor prevented from realizing their full potential; trained to think out problems and make decisions for themselves
- **in emotions:** able to cope with shyness, fear, anger, grief, love; able to make good relationships with older or younger people and with those their own age, of either sex
- **in spirit:** having made a relationship with God through Jesus Christ; knowing something about worship, prayer, the fellowship of other Christians and the church
- **in character:** to be loyal, dependable, kind, generous, ready to defend the weak, not afraid to stand up for what they believe to be true

TOO PERFECT?

No parents are likely to kid themselves that they've produced a son or daughter who is so completely ready to face life and so uniformly developed as the imaginary young person described above. In fact, it's the people with unsolved difficulties and with some underlying self-doubt or fear who are far more likely to be the achievers in life than the perfectly-balanced textbook types. Many masterpieces have been created and many crises successfully handled by men and women whose need to prove themselves to *themselves* gave them drive and will-power to endure. Any deficiency in body or mind or character can become a spur to achievement if it's accepted in a constructive way.

HANDICAPPED?

In one sense every human being is handicapped in some way. Some factor has prevented complete development in one area or another. It may be a physical weakness resulting from accident, illness or general lack of stamina. A person may be emotionally handicapped as the result of something that happened in childhood. It could have been the loss of a parent or any one of a number of frightening experiences. Human beings are unpredictable. What can be a shattering experience for one can be happily taken in his stride by another.

WHAT'S THEIR WEAKNESS?

As parents you know your child of old, and are probably well aware of his particular physical, emotional or character weakness. It may be shyness or stubbornness; there may be a childhood scar that will stay with him all his life. You may need to go on giving understanding and loving support in these areas of weakness or underdevelopment for the rest of your relationship with him. No nagging or discussion of the problem is called for unless he wishes it, but rather back-up and encouragement that will help him to come to terms with his own trouble-spots.

SHARE THE LOAD

In his letter to the Galatian Christians, Paul tells us to bear one another's burdens. But he also says that 'every man shall bear his own burden'. There are some situations where help can be given, but there is another sense in which every human being must learn to shoulder for himself the 'personality pack', or 'burden', that is his unique possession and responsibility. It is no kindness to try to relieve your adult son or daughter from coming to terms with the weakness or handicap that he alone can conquer or learn to live with courageously.

FAILURE?

Quite apart from handicap or weaknesses that your children may have been born with or have been saddled with through no fault of their own, there are also ways in which, by deliberate choice, they may have failed altogether to come up to your expectations.

A son may have wasted his schooling and ended up with a dead-end job (or no job at all) through laziness and refusal to take advice. A daughter may have made a too early and unwise marriage which has led to a bitter and unhappy relationship with her husband. Another may have thrown over parents' Christian beliefs or moral standards and have chosen a way of life in complete contradiction to all mom and dad hold to be right and of value.

These are some of the failures that can hurt parents badly and leave them with a big question mark as to what went wrong. The time for putting your child straight is past. The only choice seems to be between continuing to love them, accepting them as they are, or hardening your heart, putting up a barrier of disapproval and rejection which will cut you off from any further real communication with them.

Some parents may be afraid that if they go on loving their children, talking to them and keeping the way open, they will think their wrong behavior or past mistakes are condoned. Your children know you too well to think that. It *is* possible to accept and love the wrongdoer without being a party to his wrongdoing. Isn't that exactly what God does with us?

FAMILIES ARE FOR EVER

Once a member of a family, always a member of that family. Isn't that the joy of belonging to a family? Friends can break off relationships but family members can't. Aunt Flo may be a sore trial, and certain cousins may not be mentioned, but they still belong to you, like it or not. And that very permanence of relationship gives a sense of safety and continuance.

What is true where distant aunts or cousins are concerned is much more true of your own child. Whether by birth or adoption, he's yours for keeps. You don't chuck him on to the scrap-heap just because he hasn't turned out well, in the way you might ditch a badly-developed photo or a heavy cake. He's yours, for better or worse, and he needs to know at any and every age that, whatever happens, the family tie holds good and his relationship with you won't be broken. That way there's hope for the future.

PARENTS' RIGHTS
How many of these rights do you believe parents have to their dying day?

- the right to speak their mind—tell their child what they think of him
- the right to expect obedience to their wishes or commands
- the right to be looked after in old age
- the right to put their child straight if he isn't toeing their line

HE DIDN'T ASK TO BE BORN!

You've brought him up and you may think he owes you a lot, but isn't that for him to say? After all, parents do no more than pass on to the next generation what they in turn received from their parents. Children grow up and give, in turn, to their children. It was the *parents* who chose to have their children, with all the cost and risks that involved. They have no rights over those children once they are adult.

A generation or so back unmarried daughters, and sons too, were sometimes victims of parents who looked on them as their personal property and demanded full-time attention and service, so that even marriage had to be rejected. The pendulum has swung away from that attitude but, even so, parents need to be reminded not to stand on their own rights.

ALL CHANGE!

We never see the end of the story—for our children or ourselves. God has promised that those who give their lives to Jesus Christ will one day be like him in character. Part of that process takes place in this life, and continues till the day of death. So parents need patience and prayer as they wait to see change both in their children and in themselves. It's easy enough to think of the children as the ones who need to change and develop further, but every human being needs to go on growing if he is to become mature. If you think *you've* stopped changing, or don't need to change, think again!

GIVE AND TAKE

In a good friendship there is:

- giving **and** receiving
- listening **and** talking
- helping **and** being helped

Once your children are grown-up, a satisfying two-sided friendship can develop. After all, you have all the advantages of shared memories, shared experiences and shared characteristics. So don't think you will be the only ones to give advice, give presents, give help or to listen. Children can be advisers, confidants and listeners to *your* problems too. And if you don't *expect* any return, you can enjoy visits, cards, phone calls, unexpected gifts, treats and shared confidences as a delightful bonus. Parents and children need to accept each other on this new, mutual and equal footing.

GET RID OF GUILT

Parents can feel guilty. John's dad sees his own quick flare-ups in John's fits of temper. Val's mom recognizes her own quick tongue in her daughter's smart and hurtful repartee. Parents can feel guilty both about the traits they have passed on and the mistakes they may have made in bringing up their child. Too late they may wish they had been firmer or less disciplinarian.

Children can feel guilty too. An article in a woman's magazine dealt with the topic of women in their late twenties or their thirties who were full of guilt about parents they had never truly broken free from. Some felt guilty for ever having left home; others for having adopted a way of life of which their parents didn't approve.

Guilty feelings destroy relationships. God's forgiveness brings release, peace and a restored relationship with him. We need God's forgiveness—and perhaps our children's too—for the mistakes we made. He is able to make something good and positive even from those confessed mistakes. Children need to be relieved of their guilty feelings too, to feel that their parents no longer have a hold over them or a right to direct their way of life. Let them know that they are accepted whatever happens. In a shared experience of forgiveness, freedom and love, the relationship can go on flourishing and growing.

LOVE MEANS HURT

Bringing up a family means hard work, and cost in terms of money, effort, frayed tempers and nerves. It also means a lot of fun, laughs and shared enjoyments. It may also involve heartbreak or heartache of which your children can be totally unaware, or only dimly conscious. God took a big risk when he

created men and women with freedom to choose good or evil—
to love or reject him. Having children involves risk too. You
may follow the guide-lines wisely, yet there is no guarantee at
the end. But the attempt is worth the pain. You have helped to
create and train people with immortal souls. You have been
involved in the greatest single experiment in life. You must go
on hoping, loving them and praying for them to the end of the
road.

SOME USEFUL ADDRESSES

For further information on self-help organizations:

Self-Help Center
1600 Dodge Ave, Suite S-122
Evanston, Ill. 60204
312-328-0470
(A clearing house of information and a referral service.)

For help in answering any health question:

The National Health Information Clearing House
PO Box 1133
Washington, DC 20013
Toll-free: 1-800-336-4797
(They may not answer your question, but they will tell you who can.
They prefer phone, rather than mail, queries.)

**Catalogs and order forms for useful information
are available from:**

Consumer Information Center
Department L
Pueblo, Colo. 81009

Public Affairs Pamphlets
381 Park Avenue South
New York, NY 10016

Superintendent of Documents
US Government Printing Office
Washington, DC 20402

INDEX

Abortion 18, 78–80
ACTs 25
Adoption 103
Alcohol abuse 74–77
Allowances 63–64
Anger 45–48
Anorexia nervosa 70–71

Baptism 55

Careers advice 82–88
Career Resource Center 85
Christian Student Organizations
    colleges/universities 90, 92
    schools 30–31
Church 53–57
Church schools—see School
Church Youth Groups 54–55
Clothes 66–67
College 25
Confirmation 55–56

Depression, adolescent 33–34
Discipline 11–12, 35–37, 42–45
Dress—see Clothes
Drug abuse 74–78

Earnings 64–66
Education 21–27, 82–83, 85–86
Emotional problems 32–34
Employment 83, 100–101
    part-time 64–66
Examinations 25, 28–29

Family benefits 63–64
Food 67–70
Fostering 97–98
Friends 60
Friendship, parents and
    children 108–109

German measles 71
Getting up in the morning 53
Guilt 109

Higher education—see Education
Homework 28
Homosexual feelings 19
Hygiene 16, 71–72

Immunization 71
Independence 10–11, 34, 39–42,
    49–51, 88–90, 93–98
Interviews 87

Job choice 83–85, 86
Job, part-time for schoolchildren—
    see Employment
Job Training Partnership Act 88
Juvenile offenders 80–81

Love 11–12, 37–39, 107

Marriage preparation, for
    teenagers 17, 91–92
Marriage relationship, of
    parents 98–100
Masturbation 19
Menstruation 16–17

Nutritional needs 69

'Options'—see School, subject choice
Outside interests for mothers
    100–103

Parochial schools 22
Parents' days/nights—see School
Parent Teacher Associations 27–28
Polio, booster doses 71
Prayer 56–57
Pregnancy, teenage 78–80
Puberty, physical signs of 13–16

Quarrels—see Rows

Reading 59–60
Relaxation 58–59
Religious Education, in
    schools 22–23
Rows, family 45–48
Rubella—see German measles

SATs 25
Saturday jobs—see Employment,
    part-time
School
    assembly 23
    choice of 22
    church 22
    junior high 26–27
    open days/parents' nights 27
    subject choice 23–24
Sex education 17–21
Slimming—see Weight-watching
Smoking 75
Spare time 58–60, 98–103
Sunday 59

Television-viewing 52–53
Tetanus, booster doses 71
Tuberculosis tests 71

Unemployment 87–88

Venereal diseases 17, 18, 79
Voluntary work 101–103

Weight-watching 70–71
'Wet' dreams 15–16